THE POT THICKENS

Recipes from the Kitchens of Writers and Readers

Edited by

Victor J. Banis

The Borgo Press
An Imprint of Wildside Press

MMVII

CONTENTS

ABOUT THE EDITOR

Writing as V. J. Banis, Jan Alexander, and a host of other bylines, **Victor J. Banis** is the critically acclaimed author ("…the master's touch in storytelling," *Publishers Weekly*) of more than 150 published novels (*Longhorns*, Carroll & Graf, 2007) and nonfiction works, and his short pieces have appeared in numerous journals (*Blithe House Quarterly*) and anthologies (*Paws and Reflect*, Alyson, 2006; and *Charmed Lives*, Lethe Press, 2006). Many of his books are being published by the Borgo Press Imprint of Wildside Press. A native of Ohio and longtime Californian, he lives and writes now in West Virginia's beautiful Blue Ridge.

INTRODUCTION

On The Pleasures of Cookbooks

I'm an inveterate reader of cookbooks. I can get nearly as much pleasure out of a well-planned menu in a cookbook, or an intriguing and well-seasoned recipe, as I can from the products thereof. The mention of freshly chopped basil brings its scent to my mind; a description of tomatoes simmering in wine teases my taste buds with sweet-acid sensations.

But there is more to be found in the perusal of cookbooks than gustatory pleasure alone. Cookbooks are a reflection of their culture and their time. One tome from the early fifties, for instance, prefaces a recipe with the rather breathless announcement that it came from the food service provided on Pam Am's Clipper flights. In the fifties, travel by air was the height of chic. Can you imagine anyone today boasting of an airline's recipe?

Cookbooks of the twenties and thirties call for different ingredients and sometimes use different terms—a gill, for instance, which meant one quarter of a pint, or half a cup. The modern supermarket had not yet made frozen and convenience foods readily available, and the depression made a great difference. People made "apple pies" out of crackers, used mayonnaise instead of eggs and butter to make a cake, and made countless other substitutions.

The cookbooks of the forties had their own style. The boys, and more of the girls than is sometimes realized, were off fighting to make the world safe for Jessie Helms. Rationing was in effect, so cooks needed tips on getting by without rationed or hard to find items. Convenience foods had begun to appear on grocery store shelves but for the most part were still largely in the future, and so were most of the home appliances and gadgets we take for granted today—no microwaves, convection ovens, home dehydraters, Cuisinarts, juicers. Even the blender was a rarity. The lowly pressure cooker counted as up-to-the-minute kitchen gear. In the winter, unless you happened to live in Florida or California, fresh fruits and vegetables were rare, and expensive, and you hardly saw them mentioned at all in recipes. Tomatoes meant canned tomatoes, generally, home-canned.

The fifties were the era of the casserole. Television was new, and very big, though the screens were small. The TV dinner soared to undreamed of heights of popularity, but the casserole—cooked in one dish, with little attention needed, so freeing the cook to join her guests in watching Toast of the Town—wasn't far behind. WWII and exposure to other cultures had opened the minds of meat-and-potato Americans, though "sophisticated" cooking at the time as often as not meant a can of Cream of Mushroom soup as a sauce. The more adventurous cooks thinned it with a bit of wine, and maybe added an herb or two. But there was some very good food, too. James Beard was the champion of American cooking, and the James Beard Cookbook is still, in my opinion, one of the very best basic cookbooks, suited to beginners and serious cooks alike.

With the sixties, the American palette became more sophisticated. Julia Child was suddenly the darling of the kitchen, and adventurous cooks followed in her wake, whipping up theretofore unheard of sauces and baking their own croissants. Other celebrity cookbook writers and chefs jumped on the bandwagon, and so did the makers of kitchen appliances. More Americans were traveling abroad, and bringing gustatory pleasures back with them. American cooks came of age, in a sense, although I take umbrage at the suggestion that American food and cooking was not already quite good, in its own way. It was simply that in the sixties and seventies, it grew up. Italian cooking, for example, was no longer a matter of covering everything with the heavy red "gravy" that was familiar to earlier generations of Italian-Americans (and which, nonetheless, can be quite tasty) but now meant sauces as light and elegant as anything found in French cuisine (which, in fact, developed from Italian cooking, though the French do not like to say so.)

Today, there are entire television channels devoted to cooking shows, some of whom have made stars of their hosts and hostesses. Even the most plebian home has cooking gadgets that would have been unimaginable a generation or two earlier and it is a rare home-cook who cannot do a carbonara or a pesto sauce.

I have long believed, however, that there is a bit of the princess and the pea in much modern cooking. You may call it boeuf bourguignon, my dear, but it is still a beef stew. I recall a cookbook I once read that was a collection of recipes from the kitchens of grand

English estates, one of which called for "foot sugar"—I never was quite clear on that—and another said to "put a bowl on the floor next to your tallest ladder, have the butler climb the ladder with a pitcher of cream and pour the cream into the bowl from the highest rung." Well, yes, I suppose that could work—or, you could just beat the hell out of that cream with the wire whip found in almost every kitchen today.

So, I have tried to keep this one simple. There are recipes here that even those individuals who insist they cannot cook should be able to manage (check out Welsh Rabbit in the section on brunch dishes), and others that are meant for the serious cook (*Boeuf à la mode*, in the beef section, and as I once told a school classmate, you'll be glad you did it—although, I confess, we were not in the kitchen), and I have tried to identify them. And since I am diabetic, and am cursed with a sweet tooth as well, I have even included a special section of diabetic-friendly desserts, all of which have passed the taste tests with friends both diabetic and non.

Many of these recipes come from friends in a wonderful online writers group, gaywritersreaders, and some of them from my own extensive collection and others from friends and relatives. I hope that you will find them useful, and that they will inspire you to spread your wings, and provide those of you who are nervous about cooking to do more of it. If you follow a good recipe carefully, you will almost always find that you have produced something you and others will enjoy, and after all, isn't that much of what life is about?

Some notes on using the recipes (you probably should read this before progressing, but they're your buns):

Unless otherwise specified, flour means all purpose flour (unbleached is better.) Some recipes call for Self Rising Flour. You can buy that at your market, or you can make your own by adding 1 ¼ teaspoons baking powder and ⅛ teaspoon salt to each cup of all purpose flour. So, if a recipe calls for 2 cups self-rising flour, you would add 2½ teaspoons baking powder and ¼ teaspoon salt, but note that you have changed the total quantity of the flour, and should adjust that as well. In other words, stir the flour, baking powder and salt together thoroughly in a bowl, and then carefully spoon out 2¾ teaspoons and discard, and you are now adding the proper amount of flour to your recipe. That is not critical to every recipe, but in some, such as for cakes, exact measurements are important.

Unless otherwise specified, salt is ordinary table salt (the little girl with the umbrella); pepper should be freshly ground and I wouldn't get too excited if the recipe calls for "white pepper" or green pepper" or whatever—pepper is pepper. Sugar is ordinary table white sugar. You can use fresh and dried herbs interchangeably, though fresh will certainly be better: 1 teaspoon of a dried herb is generally the equivalent of 3 teaspoons fresh. Eggs are large, grade A. Nutritionally, white or brown shells make no difference, but the brown shells are a little firmer which, for me, means less chance of a bit of egg shell in the scrambled eggs. Milk is either whole or 2% (don't switch to non-fat unless directed); butter and margarine are generally interchangeable. (I buy unsalted because it freezes better; also, if you are sautéing in butter, salted butter burns more quickly), but do not use the light versions unless specified. Mayonnaise, cream cheese and sour cream can be either regular or low fat (light), but not non-fat unless the recipe calls for it. Note that light mayonnaise does not hold up quite as well as regular, and may "weep" in a dish that sits overnight. Unless you want to make your own mayonnaise—and far be it from me to discourage you—buy Hellman's, which is sold in some parts of the country as Best Foods. For plastic wrap, I specify Saran, because I find it the most satisfactory. If you have room, keep it in the freezer, it will be less cantankerous. Oh, and when it inevitably sticks to itself on the roll and you can't find the end, use a soft, clean toothbrush, lightly, or a vegetable brush.

Olive oil and grapeseed oil are the healthiest oils (and canola oil, but only if it is cold pressed) but olive oil has a distinct flavor not suited to all dishes, and it burns at a lower temperature, so grapeseed oil is your best bet for cooking at high temperatures or where a more neutral flavor is desired. Olive oil—da Vinci is a very good oil at a modest price. If you want to splurge (and I think it's worth it) go for Columela Extra Virgin, from Spain. The only grapeseed oil I can get locally is Carapelli, from Italy. It is excellent.

When it comes to baking and desserts, vanilla is one of the most critical ingredients. If you want the good stuff—and if you don't, you might as well close this book here and put it aside, we are simply not on the same wave length, sweets—it is going to be expensive. There are a number of reasons for this, but suffice to say that the bean comes from a type of orchid, and must be harvested while the orchid is in flower, and since the flower often lasts only a single day, the beans must be harvested by hand daily, which makes the process very labor intensive. There are many opinions on which is the best vanilla. Some want the stuff from the Mexican village of Papantla, where it originated, and that is excellent, but, if you buy vanilla directly from Mexico, rather than in this country, be sure that the label says "no coumarin," which is banned here because it is not healthy. There are those who say the best vanilla comes from Tahiti, and some think the Bourbon island (hence, the designation Bourbon on vanilla bottles, which has nothing to do with the booze) of Réunion. All Bourbon vanillas come from the Indian Ocean islands, such as Madagascar. If you stick with Bourbon vanilla, you will be fine; if you want the very best, look for Réunion Island, or Papantla on the label.

A little common sense: garlic cloves and onions, among other things best not mentioned in a cookbook, come in many different sizes. If a recipe says, "1 garlic clove, minced," or, "one small onion, chopped," it means the exact amount is not essential. If it says, "1 teaspoon minced garlic," or "½ cup chopped onion," it probably is.

Here is a little tip that will ultimately save you all kinds of time and work: get into the habit of measuring your herbs and spices—salt, *e.g.*—first in a measuring spoon and then dump it into the palm of your hand and take a good look at it. If you do this a few times, you will soon find that you can "measure" a teaspoon or a half teaspoon of whatever just by pouring the right amount into your hand.

Equipment: I mentioned that wire whip or whisk above. I use a big balloon one for beating egg whites and cream, but for most sauces, I use a small flat bottomed version, which I find eliminates the need for heating the milk or adding it slowly, as called for in most sauce recipes, since my whisk's flat tush reaches the entire bottom of the pan, "corners" included, and by whipping briskly you can avoid lumps or burning; and you generally don't have to "stir constantly," as many recipes say. These flat bottom whips can be difficult to find, but they do show up in some cooking stores, and when I find them, I generally buy two or even three, so I always have a supply. I particularly like one from the German manufacturer, Rosle, which is a bit more expensive than some, but comes with a lifelong guarantee, and you can probably find this online. You can certainly get by without one of these, but if you can find one, I think that you will soon fall in love with the savings in time and work.

The best garlic press is the Zyliss Jumbo. Or you can waste your money on another one if you prefer.

Too many people today think they just haven't the time to cook properly. Nonsense. Some of these recipes do involve a serious commitment in time and effort, but many of them take scarcely longer than whipping together something out of a box (and, indeed, I have had no qualms about including dishes that start with convenience foods). If time really is an issue—say, you work days and have to put dinner together in short order when you arrive home; or, you like to sleep in on Sunday morning, but he wants breakfast—get into the habit of reading through a recipe to see what can be done ahead. Many casseroles and stews can be made ahead, and even where a dish must be finished at the time of serving, you can have most of the ingredients chopped, diced, measured, *etc.*, the evening before and stored in plastic bags or containers, and when you get in from work, have not very much to do to put a casserole together. Or, for instance, look at the Mayo Biscuits in the section on Breads. There are only three ingredients. You can measure and combine the milk and the mayonnaise the night before and put them in the refrigerator in a pint jar with a lid, and measure out the flour in a large mixing bowl, cover it with foil or Saran, and let it sit on the counter, and in the morning, it will take you no more than a minute to whip it all together, less time than it would take you to open one of those refrigerated packages of biscuits, which would not be half so good. There is an omelet, as well, in the Eggs and Brunch section, which can be entirely assembled up to two days before cooking; and Victor's Brunch Casserole is also assembled the day before and cooked, with no attention from you, while your brunch guests have a drink. What could be simpler than that? Skip the excuses and start cooking.

A final observation: I see that the longest section in the book is the one for desserts, and the longest "recipe" the one for martinis. I will leave you to interpret that as you will.

—Victor J. Banis
2007

►*Appetizers, First Courses, and Hors D'oeuvre*

Some of these are meant as first courses to precede a meal, and others are intended to be served at a cocktail party, or with drinks before dinner. There are entire cookbooks on this course, but these are some varied and delicious examples. If you are a neophyte having your first cocktail-do, there are some truly delicious dips and spreads available at your supermarket. Don't be shy about using them. If you like, spoon them from their original containers into pretty bowls, and garnish with chopped parsley, rounds cut from the green tops of scallions, or even some toasted pine nuts, and serve with an assortment of crackers or raw vegetables. You can also put out some bowls of nuts, and even two or three kinds of cheese on a platter, with a sharp knife and again, lots of crackers. And, when you are feeling a bit more adventurous and are over the "I've-never-done-this-before" jitters, then try some of these recipes, many of which are easy indeed.

TRIPLE CRÈME SHORTBREAD

These are a wonderful accompaniment to cocktails. Don't be worried about the strong taste or aroma of the cheese. It mellows out completely when the shortbreads are cooked. The only problem is that people often assume they are sweet cookies. You could garnish each with a leaf of an herb—one parsley leaf, for instance, or a single sprig of rosemary, or sprinkle them lightly with a little black pepper. My friend Bruce suggested adding a pinch of one herb or another to the recipe, which I think is an excellent idea.

1 cup (about 10 ounces untrimmed weight) Saint Andre or other triple crème cheese, at room temperature and trimmed of rind (if you don't know what a triple crème is, ask at the cheese shop, or just buy a good brie.) It is easier to trim the rind while the cheese is cold, then bring it to room temperature.
¼ pound (1 stick) unsalted butter, at room temperature

1 teaspoon minced garlic, optional (the easiest way to do this is to put the peeled garlic cloves through a garlic press, preferably the afore-recommended Zyliss Jumbo)
2 cups unbleached all purpose flour

Combine cheese, butter and garlic in food processor and blend until creamy. Add flour and process just until the dough comes together and forms a ball. Using the palms of your hands, form dough into two 2-inch diameter cylinders, wrap separately in Saran wrap and refrigerate until well chilled, preferably overnight. Preheat oven to 350. Slice dough into rounds about a generous ¼ inch thick (or a skimpy ½ inch) and place about 2 inches apart on cold, lightly greased baking sheets. Prick the top of each cookie 2–3 times with the tines of a fork. Bake until they just begin to turn golden around edges, about 15–20 minutes Tops should not brown. Immediately remove and cool on wire racks, then store in airtight container.

ROSEMARY WALNUTS

A delicious nibble with drinks. If you are touchy about spicy foods, just skip the cayenne, or replace it with garlic powder. My friend, Ginger, likes to toss these on a salad (at the last minute, so they don't get soggy). Oh, they can be frozen and just set out to come to room temperature when you are ready for them.

2½ tablespoons unsalted butter
2 teaspoons dried rosemary, crumbled (or another herb)
1 teaspoon salt
½ teaspoon cayenne
2 cups (about 8 ounces) walnut halves

Put rack in middle of 350° oven. In the oven, melt butter in a baking sheet with sides, stir in rosemary, salt and cayenne. Toss walnuts to coat well and spread in one layer. Bake 10 minutes, serve warm or at room temperature

ROASTED ASPARAGUS WITH PROSCIUTTO

This is really more a first course for a nice dinner than a cocktail go-with, but it could make a nice brunch dish with just some fruit and some good bread.

1 pound fresh asparagus, about 19 stalks
Olive oil
About ½ pound prosciutto, sliced as thin as the deli can slice it (yes, it will be falling apart, but if it is not very thin, it is too chewy to eat.) Don't worry about leftover prosciutto. Drape if over a slice of melon or a pear or a peach, or dice it up and add to some scrambled eggs. Mail it to me if nothing else.

Preheat the oven to 400 degrees. Snap ends off the asparagus (hold at each end and break; it will break where the stem begins to get tough. Discard the bottom end) Wrap each stalk in a slice of prosciutto, drizzle lightly with olive oil, sprinkle with salt and pepper and roast about 15 minutes. Serve warm or at room temperature.

POTTED SHRIMP

If you like a firmer result, you can use additional butter, up to two sticks; this will be more like shrimp butter, of course, and still very good, but maybe just a tad less healthy for your arteries.

1 pound shrimp, shelled, deveined, and cooked until just done, drained and rinsed (or, if your market has a reliable seafood counter, buy them already cooked and peeled; ever so much easier; but they sometimes leave the tail shell on, and of course you will want to remove that)
1 stick unsalted butter, cut into cubes
1½ teaspoons lemon juice
1 teaspoon minced onion
¾ teaspoon salt
½ teaspoon Worcestershire sauce
½ teaspoon Tabasco or other hot sauce
½ teaspoon anchovy paste
¼ teaspoon fresh pepper

Place shrimp and butter in food processor and blend until smooth. Add remaining ingredients, blend until smooth and well mixed. Season with extra salt if needed. Scrape into serving bowl and smooth the top. Serve immediately or refrigerate and set out 2 hours before serving with an assortment of party crackers or toasts.

SHRIMP SALAD

You can serve this with crackers or cocktail breads, but it is especially nice on Belgian endive leaves. For a party, I put the shrimp salad in a bowl with a spoon, and surround it with the leaves, and let the guests spoon it onto the leaves themselves.

8 ounces medium shrimp, cooked and finely chopped
3 ounces goat cheese, at room temperature
2 to 3 tablespoons (more or less) chopped chives
¼ cup chopped celery
1 tablespoon lemon juice
1 tablespoon (about) of mayonnaise
Coarse salt and ground pepper

Combine shrimp, cheese, celery, about 2 tablespoons of the chopped chives, and the lemon juice, season with salt and pepper, and toss with just enough mayonnaise, about 1 tablespoon, to bind it all together. Cover and refrigerate for up to one day. When serving, garnish with an additional sprinkle of chopped chives.

MARINATED ANCHOVIES

Absolutely delicious. I like to fix these for a cocktail party because many people don't eat anchovies, so there is always lots for me—though if anything could change their minds, this would be it, and often someone who says they cannot bear anchovies changes their mind after trying this. And it's very pretty on a buffet table.

2 (two ounce) cans or jars of anchovies in olive oil, drained, and
    save the oil (needless to say, the very best you can find; the exact
    weight isn't critical)
1 tablespoon lemon juice
1 tablespoon olive oil
1 tablespoon finely chopped shallot
¼ teaspoon finely chopped garlic (you can use a garlic press, but
    minced is better in this case)
Freshly ground black pepper

1 tablespoon chopped dill
1 tablespoon finely chopped parsley
1 teaspoon finely chopped chives
1 jar roasted red peppers
12 black olives, Greek or Italian, or a mix of green and black olives
Buttered toast or slices of baguette

To the oil from the anchovies, add lemon juice, olive oil, shallot, garlic and black pepper; beat thoroughly with a fork, then stir in dill, parsley and chives. The mix should be thick but still fluid. If it seems too thick, add a little more olive oil.

Cut the roasted peppers into thirds or fourths and arrange like flower petals on a large platter, trimming as necessary to make them more flower like.

Separate the anchovies and scatter them randomly over the peppers (or arrange them like the spokes of a wheel, but I think the random scatter looks prettier). Spread the herb mixture over all and garnish with the olives. Cover loosely with waxed paper and let marinate at room temperature for at least an hour. Serve with buttered toast (and plenty of cocktail napkins.) The toast can be made ahead and reheated in 250° oven just before serving. If you must refrigerate the anchovies, let them return to room temperature before serving.

LOUISVILLE BENEDICTINE SANDWICH SPREAD

This can be thinned with sour cream or mayonnaise and used as a dip; or combine in sandwiches with bacon or sprouts. It was originally intended, however, for dainty tea sandwiches, and they make a convenient finger food for a party.

6 ounces of cream cheese, at room temperature to soften
1 medium cucumber, peeled, seeded and grated
1 medium yellow onion, peeled and grated (you can do both the onion and the cucumber in the food processor if you have one)
2 tablespoons of mayonnaise
¼ teaspoon Tabasco
Salt
Green food coloring, if desired.

Place cream cheese in bowl and mash with fork until smooth, or whip it in a food processor. Wrap cucumber in cheesecloth or a clean dishtowel and squeeze out and discard juice. Add cucumber to cream cheese and mix thoroughly. Wrap onion in cheesecloth or clean dishtowel and squeeze juice into cream cheese mix, then discard onions. Mix mayonnaise and Tabasco into cream cheese. Season to taste with salt and add 1 drop of green food coloring, if desired. Spread on thinly sliced white sandwich bread trimmed of crusts, top with another trimmed slice and cut into finger sandwiches.

BETH MORGAN'S PIMENTO CHEESE SANDWICHES

For many, "pimento cheese" means those little glasses on the supermarket shelf filled with an all but inedible yellowish glop; but anyone who has lived in the South knows that what those little glasses contain bears about as much resemblance to real pimento cheese as plastic fruit has to a real apple. Nowell Briscoe is a true Southerner and a true "book person," a writer, voracious reader and friend and confidante over many years to countless writers. He is also a connoisseur of good food, evidenced by this recipe, accompanied by his story of how he came to have it:

"One thing all southerners take very seriously is a death. Whether it be a family member or a close friend, when death calls on a house in the south, friends assemble at the home and bring in an array of wonderful, delicious meals to keep the members of the family fed until the day of the funeral. They come armed with trays of fried chicken, baked beans, squash casseroles, potato salad, Jell-O salads, tomato aspic, cakes, pies, cobblers, ice cream, and sandwiches of every kind, type and description.

One of the best sandwiches I have ever tasted came from my friend, Beth Morgan, who is a gourmet cook in her own right. She brought a tray of her pimento cheese sandwiches to my home when my partner's mother died last year and when we bit into these light, fluffy pieces of culinary delight, my partner and I both looked at each other as if to say, "Oh My God, this is the best." Sadly, when word got around about the sandwiches, they began to disappear and I had to move the tray off the table and remove the bottom layer of sandwiches so we could be able to still enjoy them after the friends left. Because they were so good, they didn't last as long as I had wished but I was able to convince Beth to share her secrets with me for making the "perfect" pimento cheese sandwich."

8 ounces cream cheese, softened
About 2 cups grated sharp cheddar cheese
Hellman's mayonnaise (enough to bind)

Dash or two of Worcestershire sauce
Celery salt, onion salt, and garlic salt to taste (optional)
1 (2-ounce) jar of chopped pimento

Mix all the ingredients together and either spread directly on white bread or store in refrigerator until needed. Always make sure when you do spread on bread that the mixture is room temperature for easier spreading. Whether you like to trim off the crust or leave it on is up to you. Either way, you cannot beat comfort food as good as this.

BRAUNSCHWEIGER PÂTÉ

This is a recipe for those who think they really can't cook. It is about as easy as it gets, and it is wonderful and people will think it is far grander than it is. It is easiest to do this in a food processor, but if your braunschweiger and butter are really soft you can do it in a mixer, or you could mash it all together with a fork, but that seems like a lot of work to me.

½ pound braunschweiger at room temperature (or substitute liver-
   wurst, but braunschweiger is better)
½ cup butter at room temperature
2 teaspoons grated onion
2 tablespoons finely chopped chives
2 tablespoons finely chopped parsley
2 tablespoons cognac or bourbon

Mix all well in a food processor or mixer (see above). Pile into a pretty dish or bowl and serve directly from the dish. Or pile it onto a large dish and smooth it (more or less) with a spatula, surround with chopped parsley. In any case, cool it for an hour or two before serving, to firm up. I like to serve this with canned smoked oysters (drain, toss with fresh lemon juice and chopped parsley) and melba toast, or cocktail breads (rye is excellent) cut into halves or squares, depending on size. Don't forget toothpicks for the oysters, and a spreader for the pate. It also works very well with smoked pheasant (but I suppose duck or turkey will do, if you want to be plebian)

PARMESAN CHEESE CRISPS

These are salty but good, and talk about easy—perfect with a dry martini.

Preheat oven to 400°. Line baking sheet with parchment paper, brush lightly with olive oil and dust with flour, shaking off excess. Grate 8 ounces Parmigiano-reggiano (or other dry cheese) on the medium holes of a box grater. For each crisp, spread ¼ cup (more or less) of the cheese into a circle on parchment paper and bake until golden, 7-10 minutes. Remove baking sheet from oven, slide parchment onto wire rack and let cool—then carefully peel crisps off parchment.

GUACAMOLE WITH SALSA

Make the Guacamole:
About 1½ pound peeled and pitted avocados (about 3 large avocados)
2 tablespoons lime juice
½ teaspoon kosher salt
½ teaspoon Tabasco
1 clove garlic, pressed

Mash the avocados, but leave them a little chunky. Stir in remaining ingredients, spoon into serving bowl and top with salsa. You can add a bit of finely chopped fruit or vegetable, say a pear or an apple, to give a bit of crunch. If you make the guacamole ahead, save the seed, and push that down into the guacamole before you refrigerate it. It will help keep it from turning brown, at least for a day or so.

Make the Salsa:
1 can (14½ ounces) fire roasted tomatoes, well drained (I like Muir
  Glen organic)
¼ cup chopped onion
2 tablespoons chopped cilantro
¼ teaspoon kosher salt
1 clove garlic, pressed
1 small jalapeño chile, seeded and finely chopped

Stir all together, spoon over guacamole, serve with tortilla chips or toasted pita wedges.

PICO DE GALLO

Robert G. Schill, aka Mister Writer, offers these two intriguing recipes for appetizers. Of Pico de Gallo, he writes "the longer that one lives in a Spanish speaking culture the more one realizes that very little can be translated word for word to understand the meaning. Pico de Gallo would literally translate Beak of the Cock (or more politely, Rooster). However, this being an appetizer, the title of this recipe means 'Something at which the cocks can peck.' Speaking of roosters, cockfights are a legal sport in Puerto Rico and there is a license plate to proclaim such activity that states 'Mi deporte son los gallos.' For the well-meaning sportsmen, that translates, 'My sport is with the roosters.' But for those of us that would rather be sporting among ourselves, serve some Pico de Gallo until the main course is ready."

6 medium tomatoes
1 medium red onion
Small bunch cilantrillo*
4 ounces Puerto Rican cheese*
Salt
2 tablespoons olive oil
2 tablespoons vinegar

Dice Tomatoes and onions. Chop cilantrillo very fine. Cube cheese very small. Combine. Salt to taste. Marinate with oil and vinegar chilling in refrigerator before serving. Serve with crackers, tortilla chips or fresh toasted bread.

*Notes: cilantrillo is the type of cilantro with lacy leaves like parsley, but if you can't find it, regular cilantro will do. Puerto Rican cheese is processed so that isn't very greasy or salty. Any cheese will be a nice complement. An easy dressing substitute would be pre-packaged Italian.

APPALACHIAN BRUSCHETTA

Robert says: "This recipe was adapted for backpackers by dehydrating the vegetables. Fresh or rehydrated, it is a lip-smacking treat at any festive gathering, at home or in the woods. First tested on the Appalachian Trial in 2000 by hikers Crackerjack and Boo Hag; therefore it seemed appropriate that it be named after the testing ground. Enjoy!"

2 cups sliced cherry or grape tomatoes
¾ cup chopped celery
½ cup sliced black olives
½ cup sliced green olives
¼ cup finely chopped parsley
1 cup carrot shavings
2 to 4 tablespoons olive oil
2 to 4 tablespoons Balsamic vinegar
Salt and pepper to taste

Cut small tomatoes into halves or quarters. Chop celery and blanch with boiling water or microwave for several minutes. Slice pitted black olives or purchase them pre-sliced. Green olives work best when the brine is discarded and olives are soaked in fresh water for at least a day to remove some of the salt. Change water on the green olives several times. Peel carrots, then with the vegetable peeler make the carrot shavings or use a grater. Combine all in a large bowl, dress with olive oil and vinegar and let marinate in refrigerator for several hours before serving. Serve with crackers or toasted bread.

CROUSTADES

These aren't, of coursed, an appetizer in and of themselves, but a container in which you can put almost any savory filling you like, but I include them here because they are handy for a party, and certainly versatile.

Trim crusts from a loaf of unsliced day-old white bread and cut eight 2½ inch slices. Trim the slices into 1½ inch cubes. Hollow out each cube, leaving a shell ⅓ inch thick, and cut off the sharp edges of the corners. Brush all surfaces except the bottom with melted butter and put on a baking sheet. Bake at 425° for about 10 minutes, until golden brown. Fill these with shrimps or other fillings such as tuna salad or diced cucumbers and tomatoes tossed in vinaigrette (but allow those to drain well before filling the shells.)

STUFFED MUSHROOMS

1 package Stouffer's Spinach Soufflé, defrosted
2 tablespoons butter
3 tablespoons finely chopped onion
¾ cup water
2⅓ cup herb seasoned stuffing (not crouton style)
½ pound bulk Italian Sausage, sweet or hot (or use links, skinned), thoroughly cooked, drained and well crumbled
¼ cup grated Parmesan cheese, plus additional for garnish
2 to 3 pounds whole white mushrooms, stems removed.

Melt butter in medium saucepan, add onion and cook until translucent. Add water, heat to boiling. Remove from heat, add stuffing, stir until moistened. Add Soufflé, cooked sausage and Parmesan cheese. Stir well. Arrange mushrooms on baking sheet, fill with spinach mixture, mounding slightly. Sprinkle with additional Parmesan cheese. Bake in preheated 400° oven for 10 to 15 minutes, till lightly browned. Serve warm.

LITTLE BITES FROM ANTHONY BIDULKA

Anthony Bidulka, Lambda Award winning author of the Russell Quant mystery series, wrote: "Every boy needs his Carol Channing. We have our own version of Carol Channing in our life who recently, upon moving into the apartment of her fourth (or perhaps fifth?) husband, and nearing eighty, had the 'cooker' (aka stove) unceremoniously removed to make room for a bookshelf/wine rack. She declared it to be immensely more useful, seeing as they would be eating out from there on in. She did arrange for a toaster oven, however, for when our CC finds herself entertaining guests for cocktails before an evening out. She has taught us many ways of impressing company with 'little bites' without the use of a cooker, which over the years have included:"

MARINATED GOAT CHEESE

1 pound (500 g.) mild goat cheese, log shape, cut into 1 inch rounds
1 tablespoon Balsamic vinegar
2 cloves garlic, minced
1 tablespoon fresh thyme, or other herb of your choice
1 tablespoon fresh parsley
1 tablespoon coarsely ground black pepper
¼ cup olive oil

Arrange slices of goat cheese on serving dish. Combine remaining ingredients and pour over cheese. Marinate at room temperature for a few hours, or keep in fridge until a few hours before serving, and then set out. May be made several days in advance. Serve on toasted pita wedges or crackers.

GARLIC BRIE

Place cloves of garlic in toaster oven at medium (350° degrees) for about twenty minutes, or until garlic has softened. Serve with Brie cheese that has softened at room temperature, and with lots of crusty bread.

*See Also: **Oven Roasted Tomatoes** in the Vegetable section*

▶*Sauces, Dressings, and Salads*

MUSTARD SAUCE FOR ASPARAGUS

Asparagus mostly gets sauced with butter or hollandaise, both of which are tasty, and neither of which is especially good for you. This is a delicious alternative that can be served as well on other vegetables. Try it also on cold roast pork.

¼ cup olive oil
2 tablespoons white wine vinegar (or use half cider vinegar, half white vermouth)
2 teaspoons Dijon mustard
1 clove garlic, finely minced, or through a garlic press (much easier)
Salt and pepper to taste

Whisk everything together, or blend in a blender.

ANOTHER ASPARAGUS SAUCE

This one is particularly good on grilled asparagus.

3 tablespoons lemon juice
1 tablespoon Balsamic vinegar (or substitute 1 tablespoon cider or red wine vinegar and ½ teaspoon sugar)
1 tablespoon rinsed and drained capers
½ cup diced roasted red bell pepper (the kind in a jar at the super-market)
¼ cup chopped red onion
Salt and pepper to taste

Whisk the lemon juice and vinegar together, stir in the remaining ingredients.

BÉCHAMEL (WHITE SAUCE)

Béchamel is one of the sauces mère (mother sauces) of French cook-
ing, so called because it is the basis for literally scores of other
sauces with various flavorings (made with part stock instead of the
*milk or cream, for instance, it becomes a **Velouté**; add an egg yolk*
*and some cream and it becomes a **Sauce Parisienne**; or, with some*
*chopped tomatoes and a bit of shrimp butter, a **Sauce Nantua.**)). I*
think it is instructive for any serious cook to make, at least once, a
classic Béchamel, which involves simply whisking the ingredients
together and cooking them for a long time over low heat, stirring
often, until they thicken and the raw flour taste is completely cooked
out. The texture is something marvelous to behold and the flavor
seems silkier as well. In today's world, however, most of us rarely
have the time or the inclination to do that, and the truth is, the short
cut method works very nicely.

In making any of these sauces, I use the flat-bottomed whisk I
described in the introductory notes, which I find eliminates the need
for heating the milk or adding it slowly. Otherwise, follow the steps
below. Most recipes call for equal amounts of butter and flour, but I
find that using slightly more butter makes it easier to blend the two.

2½ to 3 tablespoons butter
2 tablespoons all purpose flour
1 cup milk (or stock for Velouté, or a combination milk and stock)
Salt and pepper to taste

Heat the milk or stock (see notes, above). Melt the butter in a saucepan over medium heat and blend in the flour, stir together for about
2 minutes, until the butter and flour foam without coloring more
than a pale yellow. Remove the pan from the heat, wait for the flour
and butter to stop bubbling, and pour in the hot liquid all at once.
Beat vigorously with a wire whisk to blend smoothly, then return to
the heat, turn the heat up to medium high and bring to a boil, stirring
slowly. Boil, stirring constantly, for 2 minutes. Add salt and pepper,
and adjust seasoning.

SAUCE MORNAY

This is just a cheese variation of the white sauce, above.

2½ to 3 tablespoons butter
2 tablespoons flour
1 cup milk
1 onion, peeled but left whole
3 tablespoons grated Swiss or Parmesan cheese, or a mix of both
3 tablespoons heavy cream
Salt and pepper

In a small saucepan, heat the whole onion in the milk until hot but not scalded; discard the onion and set aside the milk (or you can do this in a glass measuring cup in the microwave, in which case, leave the onion in the milk until time to finish the sauce, so it will better flavor the milk.) In another saucepan, melt the butter over medium heat and blend in the flour. Cook, stirring, for 2 minutes. Remove the pan from the heat and add the hot milk all at once (see above) blending it until smooth. Return to the heat and cook slowly over medium high heat, stirring constantly, until the sauce is thickened and smooth. Add the cheese and the heavy cream, reheat, stirring until the cheese melts completely and is blended with the sauce. Salt and pepper and taste for seasoning.

QUICK BROWN SAUCE

Melt 4-5 tablespoons butter in heavy pan over low heat, blend in 4 tablespoons flour and cook, stirring constantly, until golden and bubbly. Gradually stir in 2 cups beef stock or canned beef bouillon and cook. Add 1 tablespoon tomato paste, stirring, until thick. Season with salt and pepper and a pinch of thyme and simmer several minutes, stirring often.

SAUCE DIABLE

The bottled Sauce Diable from Escoffier is good, if you want to save time, but your own will be better, of course.

1 medium onion, chopped fine
2 tablespoons of butter
½ cup beef stock

1½ teaspoons cornstarch
½ cup red wine
1 teaspoon dry mustard
2 tablespoons of Worcestershire sauce
Salt and pepper
1 teaspoon lemon juice

Cook the onion in the butter until soft. Combine the stock with the cornstarch, and add it to the pan. Add the wine, mustard, Worcestershire, salt and pepper. Cook until hot through and the flavors are well blended. Add the lemon juice just before serving with steaks or chops.

HOLLANDAISE SAUCE

Hollandaise sauce (one of the emulsified French sauces—the mother sauce, of course, is Mayonnaise) is so easy to make in a blender—or better yet, one of those little mini-food processors-that I no longer make it any other way. The key thing, though, is that the blender or mini-processor has a little hole in the top through which to pour the melted butter, which makes it impossible to add the butter too quickly—the chief reason Hollandaise fails. Mind you, I'm not talking about that big 1-2 inch plastic insert in the blender lid, I'm talking about a small indented hole in the center of that. Some older blenders do not have that. If you find yourself unable to take advantage of the appropriate opening (this sometimes happens) you will just have to use a steady hand and pour very slowly. Life ever requires adjustments. Oh, if you replace the lemon juice with orange juice, you will have a **Sauce Maltaise.**

3 egg yolks
2 tablespoons lemon juice
¼ teaspoon salt
Pinch of pepper (white pepper is nice, but don't get yourself into a
    lather)
1 stick (4 ounces) of butter

Heat the butter in a small saucepan until very hot, but not browning. Put the eggs, lemon, salt and pepper in the blender jar. Cover and blend at high speed for 30 seconds. With the blender still running, start pouring the hot butter through that little hole in the top—it will go slowly. If you must do it by hand, pour by droplets to start, until about ⅔ of the butter has been added, and you can go a little more quickly then.

One stick of butter is about all you can add in the blender, but you can scrape the sauce into a warm bowl and whisk in by hand most of another stick of melted butter, if you want a richer sauce. It's your arteries.

SAUCE BÉARNAISE

You make Béarnaise sauce exactly the same as Hollandaise, but instead of lemon juice, combine the following in a saucepan: ¼ cup wine vinegar, ¼ cup dry vermouth, 1 tablespoon minced shallot and ½ teaspoon dried tarragon, with a dash of salt and pepper. Boil this down until it is reduced to 2 tablespoons. Let it cool, put it in your blender jar with 3 egg yolks, and blend. Heat one stick of butter in a saucepan until it is very hot. With the blender running, start pouring the hot butter through that little hole in the glass insert in the lid—it will go slowly. If you must do it by hand, pour by droplets to start, until about ⅔ of the butter has been added, and you can go a little more quickly then.

As with the hollandaise, you can whisk in by hand most of another stick of melted butter, if you want a richer sauce. A classic sauce for your best steak, and also wonderful on asparagus or salmon—or do your Eggs Benedict with béarnaise instead of Hollandaise.

VICTOR'S CHILI MAYO

This is terrific with roast pork or chicken. I've also slathered in on corn-on-the-bone, and, thinned down, it makes a robust salad dressing.

Combine all:
1 cup mayonnaise
2 tablespoons lime juice
2 tablespoons chopped cilantro
2 garlic cloves, minced (I put mine through a press)
½ to 1 teaspoon Chili powder, to taste

LUBACH'S CABRILLO SAUCE

At one time, Lubach's was San Diego's most respected restaurant, famous especially for grilled shrimp with Cabrillo Sauce, the recipe for which was a secret as closely guarded as any government plot. At the time, however, there was a young man with dark eyes who worked in the kitchen, and had a thing for blonds, and in no time, the recipe was mine—and so, indeed, was the young man with the dark eyes—and both proved equally pleasurable. I'm afraid the young man is no longer mine to share, but here is the recipe he purloined for the sake of love, and that, if you did not know, is a potent seasoning indeed.

Combine 1 teaspoon yellow mustard, 10 dashes Worcestershire sauce, 5 dashes Tabasco and juice of ½ lemon. Add 14 ounces of ketchup (Hunt's is the best), simmer for 20 minutes; remove from heat, and add 4 ounces of butter a little at a time, using a wire whip.

RED ROQUEFORT DRESSING

1¼ cups mayonnaise
5 tablespoons ketchup (preferably Hunt's)
¼ cup minced onion
2½ tablespoons red wine vinegar
2½ tablespoons sugar
1½ teaspoons Dijon mustard
¾ teaspoon paprika (get Hungarian, please)
¾ teaspoon salt
½ teaspoon celery salt
⅛ teaspoon pepper
1¼ cup oil
¾ cup crumbled Roquefort

Combine mayonnaise, ketchup, onion, vinegar, sugar, mustard, paprika, salt, celery salt and pepper. Add oil in a stream, whisking, whisk until well combined (or do this in a blender, following the instructions for Hollandaise Sauce. Add Roquefort, stir gently and chill, covered.

RED WINE VINAIGRETTE

This is a fairly strong dressing, perfect with robust greens like watercress and endive.

2 tablespoons Dijon mustard
2 tablespoon red wine vinegar
6 tablespoons olive oil

Mix the mustard and the vinegar together thoroughly. Whisking constantly, slowly add the olive oil until thick and creamy (or do it in a blender).

THE LEGENDARY RED DRESSING FROM THE MONROE, GEORGIA V.F.W.

Nowell Briscoe sends this fondly remembered recipe, along with a glimpse into small-town Georgia life at an earlier time:

"A small Georgia town located right outside of Atlanta, Monroe was not a thriving city like some. The town had its "main street" with all the merchants selling their wares and during the week, plenty of parking places. It was only on the weekends that the town really came alive; folks from the country came to town to shop, the farmers came in to sell their wares and the children of the time, the '50s, '60s and '70s, would always make their way to town to see if they could spot a stranger. At that time, there was only one 'main' restaurant, the B&M Cafe on Main Street. It opened early in the mornings during the week and on Saturdays to offer their customers the 'best of the best' that could be had from the bounties of vegetables and meats, which were supplied during that time from the farmers out in the country.

"For those citizens of Monroe whose palate required a more 'refined' sort of meal, there was the 'house on the hill' on the Atlanta Highway; the 'house' being the home of the VFW. The VFW Building was nothing more than two concrete block buildings that were joined together in the back by a large room that went from corner to corner, and used mainly for the veterans, for weekly meetings or family events. On the right as you came in was a reception room, and on the left was, dare I say it—a bar where beer, wine and other horrible things like slot machines were offered to those who

wished to come out on a week night, have a beer and try their luck at the one armed bandits.

"Back in the late '50s, a man known to everyone as Junior, who was the father of one of my classmates and who was already known around town as a cook, decided to open up the large room during the weeknights as a dining room and soon enough, on Friday nights, a large majority of the town came for dinner at 'the house on the hill' and, heaven forbid, an evening of Bingo! You paid a $5.50 cover when you came in, which bought you a delicious meal and a game of Bingo afterward. As a young boy escorted by my aunt who was a Bingo freak, I spent many Friday nights at the VFW, eating and playing Bingo. I even won a couple of games, which always added greatly to my allowance of the week.

"Junior, the cook, had magical skills when it came to cooking a rib-eye steak. When you ordered the rib-eye steak dinner, you got a crisp, cold salad, iced tea, the steak, rolls and usually a peach, apple, or blackberry cobbler, depending on what fruit was in season at the time. Being a southerner, I have had my share of steaks in my time, but no steakhouse I have found since ever captured the taste, the smell, and the texture of the steaks that Junior cooked. No one, not even his family, could ever say what it was that Junior did to make his steaks so tasty.

"But, while the steaks were famous in their own right, it was another one of his concoctions that captivated my taste buds and has remained a staple in my kitchen to this very day. Before the steaks were served, you were presented with a crisp, cold salad, accompanied by Ritz Crackers and three different dressings to choose from. The first time I tasted their 'Spicy Tomato Dressing,' I was hooked! Never had I ever tasted anything that was as delicious and tantalizing as this 'red dressing,' as the folks in the kitchen called it. Some Friday nights when I went there for supper and Bingo, I asked for (and usually got) not one but two salads, just so I could savor the taste of that wonderful red dressing. Sometimes after the salad was only a memory, there I was, crumbling my Ritz crackers into the bottom of my salad bowl and pouring the red dressing over them just so I could get a little more of the dressing. It was that good!

"The popularity of Junior's weeknight dinner-club spread and for almost thirty years it flourished, Monday thru Saturday nights. Never once did I ever have a bad meal from Junior's kitchen. Junior had a slight propensity for a nip or two at night and many of his customers decided that the quality of his cooking was derived from the amount of alcohol he consumed during the evening, but no matter how much he drank, Junior always produced quality meals.

In the early '80s, with more of the Atlanta influence coming towards Monroe, the popularity of the VFW Dining Room began to wane as citizens were faced with more choices. Junior was getting up in years and the copious amounts of alcohol consumed on a daily basis had begun to take its toll on his health. At long last, the doors of the dining room closed for the last time, despite the clamor from those die-hard customers who demanded still more of the wonderful steaks—but if truth be known, what they really wanted was the highly coveted recipe for the 'red dressing.'

"There was only one lady who had made the dressing each week and when she died, it was thought the recipe went with her, but one afternoon in the summer of 1981, one of my childhood friends called all in an uproar to tell me that finally the secret had been solved. In going through the papers of the lady who made the dressing for so long, the ingredients for the recipe had been found— written on the back of a brown paper bag and stuck inside the cookbook which was her mother's.

"A sample batch was prepared and glory be, the red dressing which topped so many of those crisp garden salads was back! However there was one small difference: the soup base that had been used originally was Sexton's Tomato Soup. Sexton's is no longer in business and the next best solution is your trusty Campbell's Condensed Tomato Soup. Having made so many batches of the red dressing since the ingredients were discovered, even now I cannot tell the difference from the old versus the new.

"As Spring approaches my home and salads begin to take their place as a cool treat for dinner, you can always be sure that you will find a Tupperware container full of the red dressing from the old VFW to pour over my salad and for me, the ONLY way to enjoy this is to make sure that the salad and dressing are accompanied by a generous helping of Ritz Crackers!!! I hope this recipe will bring you as much enjoyment and pleasure as it has me for over fifty years."

2 cans Campbell's tomato soup
1 cup sugar
1 cup white vinegar
⅔ cup vegetable oil
2 teaspoons Worcestershire Sauce
3 teaspoons dry mustard
2 teaspoons paprika
1 small to medium onion, grated

Mix all the ingredients in a blender or food processor until smooth. This recipe makes about six cups of dressing but you can cut ingredients in half. Kept in the refrigerator, this dressing will last for weeks. I find the longer you keep it the better it tastes. Make sure the salad greens are crisp and cold and ALWAYS serve this with Ritz crackers and you cannot go wrong!

(NOTE: As a diabetic, I can't have all that sugar, but I find that the recipe doesn't really suffer from cutting it back. If you do so, I suggest cider vinegar, which lends its own sweetness. And I sometimes add a clove of garlic, pressed. This is also good as a marinade/basting sauce for grilled or baked chicken. Or, you can mix with some sour cream for a zippy dip for vegetables. Or, pour it over your nude body and wear it to the next reunion—that'll make them spit out the cardboard chicken. For a killer **spinach salad***, toss a large bowl of baby spinach leaves with a roughly chopped hard boiled egg or two, toss with some of this dressing (you won't need it all) and top with some crisp bacon bits. Yum. VJB).*

BENIHANA STYLE GINGER SAUCE

Excellent on vegetables or seafood

¼ cup chopped onion
¼ cup soy sauce
1 clove garlic, minced
½ ounce gingerroot, peeled and chopped
juice of ½ lemon (about 2 tablespoons)
½ teaspoon sugar
¼ teaspoon white vinegar

Combine all in blender and blend on low speed for 30 seconds or until gingerroot and garlic have been puréed. Chill before serving. Restir if necessary.

RICE SALAD

Rice Salad is one of those dishes that seem to have disappeared from the radar, and I can't imagine why. It is a lovely dish for a luncheon or a buffet, and a delightful take-along for a picnic, and Heaven knows, it is not difficult to prepare. You can cook the rice a day ahead, if you like, and make the salad the morning of. All of these vegetable amounts are more-or-less, and you can use almost any vegetable you like—barely cooked asparagus tips are especially good. I personally prefer the nuttier taste of brown rice but white rice is the usual. It can be made with wild rice, too, or a combination of white and wild rice. In that case, I suggest replacing the vegetables with raisins and fruits, fresh or dried and reconstituted, and a sweeter dressing than vinaigrette.

4 cups cooked rice, hot
½ cup vinaigrette, your own or bottled (I like Girard's)
Salt and fresh pepper to taste
⅔ cup finely chopped scallions
½ cup finely chopped green or red bell pepper, or mix
⅓ cup tomatoes, peeled, seeded and finely chopped
½ cup finely chopped celery
½ cup thinly sliced radishes
½ cup frozen peas (don't bother to thaw unless you're serving this at once)
⅓ cup chopped parsley.

Toss the hot rice with the vinaigrette and allow it to cool. When chilled, season with salt and pepper to taste and add the chopped vegetables, and toss well. If needed, add some additional vinaigrette or some lemon juice. Sprinkle with the parsley and arrange in a bowl or on a platter, without or without salad greens.

FENNEL AND MINT SALAD

Different and refreshing, a splendid luncheon salad.

2 or 2 ½ medium Fennel (or Anise root) bulbs, trimmed (Pare off tough outer skin)
½ cup extra virgin olive oil
Juice of 2 lemons
2 teaspoons salt
Freshly ground black pepper
8-10 fresh mint leaves
Parmigiano Reggiano or Asiago cheese (about a 4-ounce chunk)

In medium size mixing bowl, Cut the fennel into paper thin slices. This is best done with what the French call a Mandoline, but they are so pricey. If your city has a Japan town, you will almost certainly find a hardware/kitchen supply store that carries the very inexpensive Benriner, which does the same thing just as well. Failing either of those, just slice the fennel as thinly as you can by hand, but it really must be thin to be chewable. Drizzle fennel with the olive oil and lemon juice, sprinkle with salt and pepper, mix gently but thoroughly.

Stack the mint leaves, roll up, and slice very thinly. Set aside.

Using a vegetable peeler or mandoline, shave off thin slices or curls of cheese and set aside.

Divide fennel mixture among 4 salad plates (on lettuce if you like, but it's not really essential.) Sprinkle with mint and top with shavings of cheese. Divine!

ENDIVE, STILTON, AND BACON SALAD

2 generous servings as a main course, or 4 modest side dishes.

4 bacon slices
3 tablespoons extra virgin olive oil
1 tablespoon fresh lemon juice
Salt and pepper to taste
4 Belgian endives (about 1 pound cut across into ¾ inch pieces
1 ounce Stilton or Gorgonzola cheese, crumbled
¼ cup fresh flat-leaf parsley, leaves only.

Cook bacon until crisp and transfer to paper towels to drain. Whisk together oil, lemon juice and salt and pepper to taste. Put endives, Stilton, and parsley into a large bowl and toss with dressing. Crumble bacon over top.

CAESAR SALAD

If ever a dish qualified for the term "ubiquitous," it is certainly The Caesar Salad. Not only the temples of Haute Cuisine, but coffee shops, department store tea rooms, cafeterias and, for all I know, Greyhound buses offer it on their various menus.

Which then poses the question: why is this dish so badly made so very often? The ingredients, after all, are neither many nor exotic: Romaine lettuce, an egg, some parmesan cheese, croutons, olive oil, an anchovy or two, a dash of lemon, the miscellaneous clove of garlic-nothing, in short, that shouldn't be at hand in all but the lowliest of kitchens. Nor should slightly boiling an egg, or tossing a salad about in a bowl, tax the talents of even a neophyte cook. Really, nothing could be simpler.

I have been served so-called Caesar Salads made from iceberg lettuce, butter lettuce, mixed lettuces and greens only peripherally related to lettuce.

I have been served salads tossed in the kitchen, Heaven alone knows how long ago, with dressings made hours, perhaps even weeks and months before-yet the very essence of the Caesar Salad is its "just-tossed-ness." Otherwise, what you are having is a Romaine Lettuce Salad with parmesan dressing; it is not a Caesar. Indeed, except for the proper ingredients of the freshest and finest quality, there is really nothing *more* than immediacy to the preparation of a Caesar Salad as God intended it prepared. (Nor are my remarks meant to be blasphemous; even a cursory reading of the Scriptures will reveal that God rated the enjoyment of food and drink well up on the scale of sensual pleasures.)

The first, and foremost, consideration in constructing a Caesar salad is, of course, the lettuce. It must be Romaine. Period! It must be torn-never cut-into bite size pieces, thus providing a multitude of surfaces to which your freshly prepared dressing will cling. The serving of the leaves whole is an unfailing sign of culinary naïveté, a warning that this is a kitchen to be regarded warily.

Eschew any preparation described as Caesar Salad that a captain, or at the very least, your waiter, does not promise to prepare and toss at your table. It is your palate, after all, that these persons plan to betray. There is no such thing as a "Caesar Salad Dressing" that can be made in advance. You might just as well bring along one of those bottled concoctions from the supermarket, it will be no worse, and might well be better. A Caesar Salad must-I repeat, *must*-be tossed on the spot and placed before the prospective diner within the instant. Any other plan of action is contrary to the laws of nature. Let us put to rest, as well, the question of anchovies. I have heard no end of stories purporting to describe the creation of the original salad, with both Yea and Nay opinions on the inclusion of anchovies. Suffice. If the very first Caesar Salad was not flavored by the addition of an anchovy or two, presumably because the chef had them not to hand, it should have been; and, no doubt, the omission was corrected by the time of the second salad, which should be historic enough for anyone.

Yes, I know, there are those who insist they cannot eat these little fishlings (though I have observed many of the same resorting without complaint to their bottles of Worcestershire.) For those individuals I offer the plan espoused by my friend, Don, who likewise disdained the anchovy, but would no more have thought of ingesting a Caesar Salad without one than of carting himself off to the office without his trousers: Start by mashing the anchovy filet in your bowl-the ideal for this would be a wooden bowl used for this purpose exclusively, but let us not pick bones, a glass bowl will do. Be merciless in your pummeling of the little devil, and leave no interior surface of the bowl unmarked by its passing. Then, discard the puréed remains, and prepare your salad in the bowl. The other ingredients will inhale the essence of the anchovy, and your salad will have that elusive, subtle, but utterly necessary sapor.

As for the rest, you need only sauté some freshly diced bread in olive oil with a clove or two of garlic. Coddle an egg—which is to say, boil it for one minute exactly. Spare me, please, warnings about salmonella. The chances are very slim, and if you are unduly worried about them, shop around and find yourself some pasteurized eggs. I can't do all of your thinking for you.

Place the washed and *thoroughly dried* pieces of romaine in your bowl, and toss them well with some more olive oil, which, needless to say, will be of the finest quality. Add the fried croutons of bread, salt, pepper, your finely chopped anchovies (if you have not resorted to the above described alternative) and a tablespoon or so of freshly squeezed lemon juice. Break your coddled egg into the bowl, quickly add a half-cup or more of freshly grated Parmesan cheese, toss once again, and serve immediately.

As I said at the beginning, nothing could be simpler. Nor more delicious. Hail Caesar!

MUSTARD SAUCE

This is a strong, pungent aged dressing for roast meats, especially pork or ham. You can use it when it is freshly made, but the flavor will be very sharp. The mustard mellows over time, and is at its best at least a week or two after it is made. Put in a sterile quart jar, cover with a lid and allow to mellow. It needn't be refrigerated, but you can certainly do so, though it will take a bit longer to mellow. Add more liquid as needed and adjust seasoning to taste when you use it. Can be stored indefinitely, and will continue to mellow as it ages.

1 cup yellow mustard seeds
3 tablespoons sugar
1½ teaspoons salt
½ teaspoon freshly ground pepper
2 teaspoons ground ginger
2 cups red wine vinegar or cider vinegar

Grind the mustard seed in a spice grinder, blender or mortar and pestle. It should be about the texture of coarse cornmeal. Place the mustard in a medium bowl and add spices. Add vinegar and stir well to combine. Let stand 2 hours or more and stir again. If it is too thick, add water or additional vinegar, white wine or even dry sherry. This can be eaten at this point, but it will be very sharp (see above)

SEASONING SALT

This is great rubbed onto beef before roasting, or I have used it on chicken, fish and pork as well. I like to keep a jar of it on hand. I keep thinking of new things to season. Carrots, for instance, or... well, use your imagination.

4 tablespoons salt
2 tablespoons cracked or ground black pepper
2 tablespoons instant coffee granules
1 tablespoon garlic salt (or substitute garlic powder)
1 tablespoon celery salt
1 tablespoon onion salt (or substitute onion powder)

CREAM OF WHEAT COATING

An unusual and surprisingly good coating for chicken, pork chops, or whatever. No one has yet guessed what it is.

Combine all:
1 cup cream of wheat (not instant)
2 teaspoons kosher salt
1 teaspoon cayenne pepper
1 teaspoon freshly ground white pepper (I use black; life is too short
   to be fussy)

▶*Soups*

NOT YOUR PUERTO RICAN GRANDMOTHER'S SOUP

This is another recipe from Robert G. Schill, aka Mister Writer, who writes: "Developing a recipe for Puerto Rico Style soup was an interesting artistic achievement in the kitchen. Here on the island there are vegetables that are not readily available in other areas. It also brought back to mind a comment made by an ex-lover. 'You make better soup than my Grandmother.' Immediately he tried to retract the statement, probably having visions of his grandmother flopping around in her grave waving a soup ladle and swearing in Italian. So make up a batch and invite your lover's grandmother over for dinner and tell her: 'The secret to a good soup is a tasty stock'."

One pound cured ham
Several quarts water
One large onion
One green pepper
One dozen fresh cilantro leaves
Salt

One cup cubed apio root *
One cup cubed squash
One cup cubed potato
Several chopped broccoli florets
One small carrot sliced
One hand full of penis pasta (*well, that's what his recipe calls for, though he does add "when grandmother visits use elbow macaroni" VJB*)
Fresh bread
Butter

Directions:
In a large pot bring two quarts of water to a boil and add cubed ham, chopped onion, chopped green pepper, and finely chopped fresh cilantro leaves. Note: fresh cilantro will create a more flavorful stock. Let this simmer for a half hour or more. After simmering, add salt to taste. The secret is to have a nice flavorful stock before adding the vegetables and pasta.

After the stock is ready, add the cubed apio*, squash, potatoes, and sliced carrot. The florets of broccoli chopped very finely enhance the texture of the stock. Let simmer until vegetables are about half cooked, then add pasta. Stir to keep pasta from sticking together and bring pot to a full boil. When penises are flaccid and tender serve soup with buttered bread.

*Apio is the Puerto Rico version of celery. However, it is the root of the plant that is used verses the stems of the Apio Americana (American Celery). The Apio root is very tasty. Parsnips would make a nice substitute. *(Or celery root-VJB)*.

VICHYSSOISE

This classic was "invented" at the Waldorf Astoria in New York City, but it is really nothing but a chilled version of the traditional French leek and potato soup. Obviously, then, it can be served hot, but it truly shines when chilled. This is my easier rendition.

2 tablespoons butter
½ cup chopped shallots and scallions combined, about half and half
    (or you can use the traditional leeks, but I find them a bit of a nuisance and hard to clean)
⅔ cup chicken stock
1 can condensed cream of potato soup
1 cup half and half
½ cup milk
Chopped chives (for garnish)

In a large saucepan over medium heat, heat butter till hot, add shallots and scallions and cook 5 minutes; add chicken stock, heat to boiling, reduce heat to low, cover and simmer 10 minutes. Stir in soup, bring back to boil, simmer and stir 2 minutes. Add half and half and milk. Cool, then purée in blender at low speed. Chill, garnish with chives to serve.

AVOCADO GAZPACHO

A tasty variation on the theme. This can be served hot or cold, and is an excellent main course soup. Lots of possibilities for finishing it off, see below.

2 fully ripe Hass avocados (if small, get 3), peeled, seeded and diced
1 cup, more or less, peeled, seeded diced cucumber
1 medium to large tomato, chopped (no need to peel)
¼ cup chopped onion
1 cup chicken broth
2 tablespoons lemon juice, separated
Salt and pepper

Optional:
Broken tortilla chips
Cooked shrimp and or crab
Tortellini (I use cheese) or ravioli
Baguette slices, spread with garlic cream cheese spread, or not

Remove ¼ cup or so of diced avocado, toss with 1 tablespoon lemon juice and set aside. In batches, purée the remaining avocado, cucumber, tomato, onion, broth, 1 tablespoon lemon juice, salt and pepper in blender. To serve cold, spoon into bowls, garnish with reserved avocado and sprinkle with tortilla chips; or instead of the chips (I like this better) toast baguette slices and spread with cream cheese spread, and serve with soup. You can also add shrimp or crabmeat or both, for a main course, in which case you really don't want the chips. To serve hot, just heat the soup first, then add cooked shrimp and crab only long enough to warm them, and diced avocado last. You can also cook tortellini or ravioli separately and add to the soup at the last minute.

CONSOMMÉ BELLEVUE

This classic combination of chicken stock and clam juice sounds strange, but it works beautifully. The dish originated at the Bellevue Stratford Hotel in Philadelphia in the early part of the twentieth century. This is my twist on the original, and it is a perfect addition to the repertoire of even the most basic cook, because it is so easy, and makes a truly delicious start to even the most formal dinner. I once prepared this for a group, some of whom could not have shell-

fish; I found that a dry white wine made an acceptable substitute for the clam juice, with a final dash of lemon juice at the end; but it's much better in the original version.

4 cups chicken stock, fresh or canned, and skimmed of all surface fat
2 cups bottled clam juice
A pinch of ground red hot pepper (cayenne)
1 carrot, 1 stalk of celery, 1 parsnip (if you can't find parsnip, use a
    turnip)
1 large lemon
Parsley, chopped, for garnish

Peel the carrot and the parsnip. Cut all three vegetables into very thin julienne (or matchsticks) of uniform length, about 3 inches (these will rest in the bottom of your soup bowl, so adjust the length to assure that they fit in your bowls); poach the matchsticks in a cup of the stock for 2 to 5 minutes, just until they are bite-tender. Slice the lemons as thinly as possible.

Combine the chicken stock, clam broth and red pepper in a heavy 2-3 quart saucepan. Bring to a boil over high heat, partially covered, reduce the heat, and simmer for 15 minutes. Taste for seasoning and adjust as needed. Put a mix of the julienne vegetables, no more than a tablespoon or so, in the bottom of each bowl. Lay a lemon slice atop them, and ladle the soup over all (the lemon will float to the top). Sprinkle a pinch of parsley on top.

EASY BORSCHT

You don't find borscht much anymore, which is too bad. It is a nice, savory hot soup, and as a cold soup, it can be very refreshing on a steamy summer day.

2 (16 ounce) cans whole beets, drained (save ½ cup liquid)
¾ cup chicken broth
2 tablespoons coarsely chopped onion
4 teaspoons fresh lemon juice
½ teaspoon salt
⅛ teaspoon sugar
Dash fresh pepper
Sour cream or Crème fraîche
Minced chives

Combine beets and saved liquid with everything except sour cream and chives in blender and purée until smooth. Taste, adjust seasonings. Serve hot or cover and chill overnight and serve cold, garnished with a dollop of sour cream and chives.

CARO SOLES STONE COLD ORANGE SOUP

Caro writes: "Caro Soles (aka Kyle Stone) is a Canadian writer and teacher of writing at George Brown College in Toronto. She used to be a lot of other things. She used to teach languages, for instance, but writing is more fun, since the students now get the jokes. Mostly. Caro also used to be a great cook. She spent hours and hours in the kitchen, hovering over the sauce. The one on the stove, that is. But that was a decade or so ago. Now she has seen the light, and the only sauce of interest comes in a bottle. Hence the popularity of this recipe!" Caro's latest novels are Drag Queen in the Court of Death *and* The Danger Dance. *Web sites:*
www.carosoles.com and www.kyle-stone.com

2 quarts fresh orange juice
½ teaspoon ground cloves
Pinch of ginger
Pinch of nutmeg
Pinch of mace
1 cinnamon stick
2 tablespoons unflavored gelatin
½ cup of cold water
2 cups pineapple juice
2 cups good sherry (not too dry)
2 (11-ounce) cans of mandarin orange sections

Bring orange juice to boil; add spices. Simmer for an hour. Remove cinnamon stick. Soak gelatin in cold water to dissolve and add to hot juice. Combine the remaining ingredients and pour into glass or stainless steel container. Cover and refrigerate overnight. *(Note: an aluminum saucepan may give the O.J. a greenish cast, though the soup will still be delicious. If you have one, a non-reactive saucepan—i.e., not aluminum—will leave you a prettier soup—VJB).*

CUCUMBER SOUP

This too can be served warm, but I like it better chilled.

2 tablespoons butter
3 cups roughly chopped cucumbers (peeled and seeded first)
⅔ cup chopped green onions (white and green parts)
2 tablespoons all purpose flour
2 cups chicken broth
2-3 tablespoons dry vermouth
Salt and pepper
¼ cup half and half
Cucumber slices for garnish, if desired (or garnish with sprigs of
   dill)

In large pot over medium high heat, melt butter and cook cucumbers
and onions until translucent and tender, stirring frequently. Blend
flour well into pan juices. Gradually stir in broth and vermouth,
cook until mixture thickens and begins to boil. Taste and add salt
and pepper as desired. Cover and simmer over low heat 10 minutes,
stirring occasionally. Cool, purée in blender or food processor in
batches, stir in half and half. Serve warm or cold.

QUICK SEAFOOD BISQUE

*I always give this recipe to friends who insist they can't cook. It is
easy to make, delicious and fool proof. If you really can't cook, and
want to have someone over for luncheon, serve this with some good
crusty bread and buy one of those ready rinsed packages of salad at
the market and toss at the last minute with a good bottled vinaigrette
(I like Girard's or Good Seasons bottled vinaigrette). I have specified chopped parsley for garnish, but it can be another fresh herb,
such as dill or, especially lovely, tarragon; but fresh chopped parsley is better than dried anything. This will serve 4 as a first course,
or two very generous bowls for luncheon. If you buy cooked shrimp
at your market, be sure to remove the tail shells, as they are difficult
to deal with while you are eating the soup. Canned seafood is never
as good, but if you've nothing else to hand, drain it and rinse it well,
and let it sit for 15 minutes or so in some white wine or vermouth—
champagne, even cheap champagne, works particularly well if you
have some open anyway, but I wouldn't open a bottle just for this*

purpose. Drain the shrimp again. The wine will get rid of that iodine smell that canned seafood often acquires.

1 can Campbell's tomato soup
2 tablespoons out of a can of Campbell's pea soup (save the rest for your own luncheon one day)
¾ cup of chicken stock
½ cup heavy cream
½ cup more or less of crabmeat, or cooked shrimp, or cooked lobster, or any combination thereof
¼ cup dry sherry
1 tablespoon fresh lemon juice
Chopped parsley, about 2 tablespoons (see above)

In the top of a double boiler over simmering water, stir the first 4 ingredients together to blend well (the pea soup is lumpy). Add the crab and the sherry, and heat. Just before serving, stir in the fresh lemon juice and ladle into bowls or cups, garnish each with the chopped parsley.

RICK R. REED'S GREEN AND GOLD COMFORT SOUP

I am as much a fan of Rick Reed's recipes as I am of his devilish tales. Here is a good example of why. Rick writes, "As a horror writer, I spend my days plotting the most grisly of scenarios. One does get tired of bloody murder, dismemberment, sexual perversion, fangs, ghosts, demonic possession and worse! So when I go into the kitchen to make dinner, I want comfort food. Something that will transport my soul away from the violent world I create on the page. Here is one of my favorite, and most comforting, recipes. This soup, a green salad, and a loaf of crusty bread can make the most evil of souls forget all about haunting, possession, or even cold-blooded murder."

3 medium Yukon Gold potatoes, peeled and diced
3 carrots, peeled and diced
3 green onions, sliced (save green tops for garnish)
2 cloves garlic, finely minced
1 tablespoon butter
4 cups chicken or vegetable stock, warmed
1 cup grated extra sharp Cheddar cheese

Melt butter in large pot over medium heat. Add vegetables. Cook, stirring, until softened, about three minutes. Add warmed stock and simmer for twenty minutes. Remove from heat. With a potato masher, lightly mash vegetables to a creamy, chunky consistency. Stir in cheese. Serve garnished with onion tops.

Rick R. Reed is the author of the novels Obsessed, Penance, A Face Without a Heart, *and the short story collection*, Twisted: Tales of Obsession and Terror. *His short fiction has appeared in nearly twenty anthologies. In 2007 watch for the novels* IM, In the Blood; *and* Deadly Vision: Book One of the Cassandra Chronicles. *Rick lives in Miami with his partner, where he is at work on a new novel. Visit him online at: www.rickrreed.com.*

A SIMPLE CLAM CHOWDER

2 slices bacon, chopped
1 medium onion, chopped
1 medium potato, cubed
1 (7-ounce) can minced clams, juice drained and saved
2½ cups milk
Salt and pepper
Butter

Fry bacon and onion until onion is tender. Add the potato and the juice from the clams and enough water to cover the potato. Simmer till potato is tender, 10-15 minutes. Add clams, 2½ cups milk (or combine milk and cream as you will), salt and pepper, heat, and serve, ideally with a pat of butter on top of each serving.

PORTUGUESE SAUSAGE AND KALE SOUP

This pretty much makes a meal with some good, hearty bread.

6 ounces Lingüiça (or substitute Kielbasa or Chorizo if you can't find that)
1 large onion, chopped
1 clove garlic, chopped
1 teaspoon olive oil
½ pound fresh kale, stems discarded, leaves chopped (or use frozen, thawed and drained, see recipe instructions below)
2 cans (13¾ ounces each) chicken broth
3 cups water (with a splash of vermouth)

2 carrots, sliced
1 teaspoon dried marjoram, crumbled
Salt and pepper
½ cup uncooked long grain white rice, or other rice

Sauté Lingüiça, onion, and garlic in oil in large pot over medium low heat until tender, about 10 minutes. Add chicken broth, water, carrot, marjoram, salt and pepper, and *if you are using fresh kale*, add it now. (If you are using frozen, you will add that later.) Bring to boil, lower heat, cover and cook 15 minutes. *If you're using frozen kale*, add it now with the rice, bring to boil again, cover and simmer 15 minutes longer or until rice and kale are tender.

▶ *Beverages and Drinks*

THE MARTINI

The martini is the king of cocktails. It originally called for gin, but today is as likely to be made with vodka. Here are the directions for making a martini that I included in my memoir, Spine Intact, Some Creases, *much as they appeared there—but, I was accused by one reader of being verbose on the subject, and in the spirit of reasonableness, I have eliminated an entire sentence, though admittedly it was only a short one.*

The martini is not a difficult drink to make, requiring only a good quality gin or vodka, a few drops of a good dry vermouth, an olive with, if you like, a drop or two of its juices (which makes it a **Dirty Martini**) or if you prefer a twist of lemon peel, and lots of ice. With an onion, it becomes a **Gibson.** Some old recipes call for a drop or two of Angostura bitters, and I think that is an interesting variation, but you must be especially careful with a vodka martini to add no more than a drop, otherwise it will overpower the drink, when what you want is a very subtle effect.

I won't even dwell upon those establishments that attempt to make this noble concoction with rotgut booze, but those of you who have not read the unexpurgated version of Dante's Inferno may not know that there was a special circle in Hell set aside for just such miscreants. This detail was eliminated from the revised edition under pressure from the liquor industry and the publisher's marketing people, so you will just have to take my word for it, but I think you know by now whether or not I am likely to exaggerate.

A more common sin of bartenders—and Dante knew what to do with them as well, you may be sure—is to interpret the request for a dry martini as meaning straight gin or vodka. That is not a martini, alas, dry or otherwise. Something subtle and truly wondrous occurs with the blending of the two spirits, something that cannot be explained by mere chemistry alone but must be experienced to comprehend. Mind you, it wants only a few drops of the wine—and this is another all too common failing—to do the job. If you do not trust your wrist absolutely, the safest thing is to pour the vermouth into its bottle cap, a half a cap full at most, or better, a third, though you can be more generous when making a gin martini than if you have chosen vodka.

There are bartenders who, without asking and having made a perfectly good job of the proportions, spoil it all by handing it to you in a glass full of ice. This, too, is not a martini. I truly believe that a glass of ice water makes a good companion to a martini, but it should be served on the side.

On the opposite side of the coin—and there is probably no punishment commensurate with the crime—is serving a martini insufficiently chilled. A martini must be ice cold, practically gelid, and preferably served in a chilled glass so that its brisk coldness will last. And eschew, please, the deplorable habit of keeping gin and vermouth in the refrigerator to obviate the need for ice. The ice is indeed necessary. That slight dilution of the spirits with the melting ice—the clearest, purest ice you can find—smoothes the edges, as it were.

And since it is perfection that we are after here—for a perfect martini stands as one of the purest examples of perfection in a too often imperfect world—we might as well address that "shaken or stirred" business. Never mind what James Bond says. He is British and the British are very good with tea but have never quite grasped the essence of the cocktail.

Both shaking and stirring will chill a martini, of course, and I personally think that shaking became popular because it does so more quickly and we are always in a hurry, aren't we? To be sure, there are drinks that are appropriately shaken; drinks, for instance, with fruit juices in them are meant to be frivolous, effervescent, frothy even. Shake the dickens out of them

Drinks that are pure spirits, however, or nearly pure spirits—the martini, the Manhattan, the Rob Roy as examples—deserve to be stirred. If you will make two gin martinis, in separate shakers, violently shaking one and gently stirring the other, you will clearly discern two things. First, as any good bartender can tell you, stirring produces a colder drink, and the colder the martini the better. And, second, you will find that the shaken method truly does leave the gin "bruised," as evidenced by the oils you can see for yourself left floating atop the cocktail when you have poured it into its glass, while the stirred version retains that crystalline purity which is to be desired. Case closed.

THE MANHATTAN

*Another classic, the Manhattan is made with bourbon (or a premium blended whiskey, such as Canadian Club) and sweet vermouth and generally garnished with a cherry; a **Dry Manhattan** is made with dry vermouth and as a rule, garnished with a lemon twist; a **Perfect Manhattan** is made with half sweet, half dry vermouth (but, alas, I find today that you sometimes have to explain that to a bartender.) If, by the way, you change the bourbon to Scotch, the drink becomes a **Rob Roy**, which you can order in any of the variations above.*

3 ounces top shelf bourbon or blended whiskey
½ teaspoon sweet (Italian) vermouth, see above
Maraschino cherry or lemon twist—with a squeeze of lime it becomes a **Persian,** but most bartenders today won't know that.

DOROTHY PARKER'S CHAMPAGNE COCKTAIL

The legendary wit was fond of a tipple. One of these will tell you why.

1 sugar cube
2 dashes Angostura bitters
Champagne
Lemon twist

Put the sugar cube in the bottom of a champagne glass, soak it with the bitters, and fill the glass with bubbly. Top with lemon twist. Some add a splash of cognac, but I think that is *de trop* and, really, closer to a French 75.

THE MIMOSA

The Mimosa, a blend of half fresh orange juice and half champagne, is very popular today, and I suppose it is an acceptable way to use up a not-quite-wonderful champagne, but I would certainly be loathe to mess about that way with a glass of, say, Dom Perignon, having far too much respect for the good friar. However, I have been known to make a kind of grown-up Mimosa with a good cham-pagne, by adding just a few drops of Grand Marnier (an orange fla-

vored liqueur) and a sprinkling of grated orange zest. A much nicer way to start your day.

MAI TAI

This is the original from Trader Vic's where it was created. By now you may have noticed that I am a classicist where my cocktails are concerned.

2 ounces (¼ cup) dark rum
½ ounces (1 tablespoons) Curacao
¼ ounce (1½ teaspoons) simple syrup
¼ ounce (1½ teaspoons) orgeat syrup *
1 lime, halved.
Mint sprig, pineapple, and maraschino for garnish

Combine first 4 ingredients, shake well. Squeeze juice of 1 lime half over shaved or crushed ice in glass, pour drink over ice and decorate with reserved lime half, mint and fruit. More typically today the drink would be strained and served without the ice.

*Orgeat (ohr-SHAY) syrup can be tricky to find. If you don't find it in a bar supply store, substitute Torani almond syrup, or combine 2 tablespoons of **simple syrup** *(heat and stir equal parts of sugar and water until the sugar is dissolved, and cool) and ¼ teaspoon almond extract.*

TRADER VIC'S ORIGINAL SCORPION

1 scoop shaved ice
2 ounces (¼ cup) orange juice
2 ounces (¼ cup) light rum
1½ ounces (3 tablespoons) lemon juice
1 ounce (2 tablespoons) brandy
½ ounce (1 tablespoon) orgeat syrup (see above)
Ice cubes
Gardenia for garnish (pretty, but of course, non-essential)

Combine first 6 ingredients in blender until well mixed. Pour over ice cubes and garnish with gardenia (I sometimes wear mine in my hair instead).

SIDECAR COCKTAILS

Fresh lemon juice
Sugar
1 cup cognac or good brandy
½ cup triple sec or Cointreau
¼ cup lemon juice
Maraschino cherries or lemon peel to garnish

Dip rim of 4 martini glasses in shallow plate of lemon juice and then sugar. Allow to dry for 15 minutes. Combine cognac, triple sec and lemon juice. Pour some into a shaker with ice, shake well and pour into glasses. Garnish with cherry or lemon peel

SANGRÍA

This is refreshing and great for a picnic, or a luncheon on the patio. Really, you can use almost any combination of fruit.

½ lemon cut into ¼-inch slices
½ orange cut into ¼-inch slices
½ large apple cut in half, unpeeled but cored and cut into thin wedges
¼ to ½ cup superfine sugar (use smaller amount, taste, and add more if desired)
1 bottle dry red wine
2 ounces (¼ cup) brandy
Club soda—optional

Combine fruit and ¼ cup sugar in large pitcher. Add wine and brandy and stir well. Taste and add more sugar if desired. Refrigerate several hours. Serve on the rocks or if you like top off with club soda (I prefer it without).

CLASSIC BLOODY MARY

The Bloody Mary originated at the King Cole Bar at the St. Regis Hotel in New York City, where it was first called The Red Snapper. This is the original recipe and it remains, justifiably, a classic.

3 dashes Worcestershire (about ¼ teaspoon)
2 dashes black pepper

2 dashes cayenne
2 dashes salt
1 dash lemon juice
1½ ounces gin (I prefer vodka but the original did call for gin; just for fun, try it one day)
4 ounces (½ cup) tomato juice
Ice
1 lime wedge

Combine the first seven ingredients and pour over ice; garnish with lime wedge.

VICTOR'S BLOODY MARY

There are infinite variations on the Bloody Mary. This is my interpretation of the excellent one that is served at The Rotunda at Neiman Marcus in San Francisco.

Juice of 1 lime
1 large can (48 ounces) of tomato juice
8 tablespoons Worcestershire Sauce
1 small teaspoon horseradish
20 shakes of Tabasco
Celery salt
Absolut Pepper Vodka
Optional: the juice of another lime

Mix well. Dip glasses into the lime juice and then in the celery salt to frost the rim. Allow to sit 15 minutes. Garnish with cucumber slice. Put ice in glasses, pour in juice mix and gently stir in 1 shot Absolut Pepper Vodka; or, alternatively, serve the vodka in a shot glass on the side, so one can take sip the vodka and use the mix as a chaser. Optional: Add the juice of 1 more lime to the juice mix.

CLASSIC MARGARITA

3 ounces 100% Agave White or reposado tequila
2 ounces Cointreau (or Grand Marnier)
1 ounce fresh lime juice (if you are using Grand Marnier, make that 1½ ounces)

Shake all, strain. The glasses are sometimes salt-rimmed, but that is really abuse of top flight liquor. If you're making it with the cheaper stuff, then, okay.

COSMOPOLITAN

1 ounce vodka
½ ounce triple sec
½ ounce Rose's lime juice
½ ounce cranberry juice

Combine all in a shaker with ice, shake vigorously, strain into a cocktail glass and garnish with a lime wedge. You can multiply this simply by thinking of it as 2 parts of vodka to one part of everything else; *i.e.*, two water glasses of the vodka and one each of the other ingredients will make a big batch.

PIÑA COLADA

4 ounces Cream of coconut
4 ounces pineapple juice
3 ounces rum
1 cups ice

Combine all and mix in blender. Garnish with pineapple and cherry. Serves 2.

HOLIDAY EGGNOG

2 cups milk
¾ cup sugar
Pinch salt
1 vanilla bean, split lengthwise
4 eggs, separated (if raw egg whites worry you, look for pasteurized eggs)
1 cup bourbon
2 ounces dark rum
1 cup cold heavy cream
Fresh grated nutmeg

Pour milk, ½ cup sugar, and salt into medium saucepan. Scrape seeds from vanilla bean into pan, then add pod. Heat over medium heat, stirring until sugar has dissolved, about 10 minutes. Whisk egg yolks until well mixed. Slowly whisk 1 cup of the hot milk into yolks. Gradually add mixture back into saucepan, stirring constantly with a wooden spoon until thickened, about 5 minutes. Strain and set aside to cool. Add bourbon and rum, cover and refrigerate until cold. Whisk egg whites until frothy, then gradually add remaining ¼ cup sugar, whisking continuously until stiff, not dry, peaks form. In another bowl, whisk cream to soft peaks. Fold whites and cream into eggnog. Garnish each cup with nutmeg.

COQUITO-PUERTO RICAN EGGNOG

Here is an interesting variation on the eggnog theme from Mister Writer, aka Robert Schill, who writes: "Coquito is the Puerto Rican version of eggnog. Coconuts are plentiful at Christmas time but more labor intensive than the canned tropical ingredient. And for those who want to pass a little Caribbean cheer, coquito is the perfect drink. The use of genuine Puerto Rican rum with a bit of brandy will definitely produce a cheerful greeting for your holiday guests. Giving coquito as a gift to a friends or relatives is a holiday tradition on the island."

4 cans evaporated milk
2 cans sweetened condensed milk
2 (15 ounce) cans cream of coconut (Coco López)
12 egg yolks
1 tablespoon vanilla *(see my introductory notes—VJB)*
½ cup (4 ounces) brandy or cognac
1 quart of White Rum
Cinnamon (add this to your taste, starting with 2 teaspoons)

Mix all of these ingredients in a blender, a little at a time. You want this to come out smooth. You'll be adding this mixture to a larger glass bowl, so that you can fit everything! When you've finished blending, stir what's in the large bowl, and begin to pour into glass bottles. You will need five regular size 750 ml. bottles to store this recipe.

Tip: Make sure you refrigerate this! Remember you're dealing with raw egg yolks, just like normal American eggnog. *(N.B.—you can find pasteurized eggs in many mainland supermarkets, which eliminate the risk of salmonella; but you will still need to refrigerate this. VJB).*

LIME FREEZE

Someone reading this manuscript asked if I ever drank anything that didn't have alcohol in it. Yes, I especially like this refreshing alcohol free drink (though of course if you chose to add a bit of vodka to it, I would never tell anyone.) You can also make this with any flavor sherbet and juice you like—orange, e.g., is very nice.

2 cups softened (but not fully melted) lime sherbet or sorbet
1 cup lime juice (freshly squeezed is better but not essential)
¼ cup milk
1 sprig of fresh mint

Put sherbet, juice and milk in blender and blend for 15 seconds or just until smooth. You may have to stop the blender and stir it up a bit to help it combine. Pour into tall, chilled glass. Place a sprig of mint on the top.

BITTERS AND SODA

You can make a very refreshing non-alcoholic drink (and fool everyone else into thinking you're really having a cocktail) by filling a glass with ice, pouring club soda over it, adding 2-3 shakes of Angostura bitters, or to taste, and a squeeze of lime. Pretty, and very nice on a hot afternoon.

ORANGE JULIUS

For many years, the Orange Julius stand was a familiar sight up and down the West Coast, and many tried to discover the recipe for the eponymous orange drink. This recipe comes from a former executive with the company, and is probably about as close as one can get. This, too, is alcohol free, Mister Smarty.

1½ to 2 cups crushed ice
1 cup orange juice (fresh is best, or use frozen reconstituted)
1 tablespoon vanilla pudding mix (or custard mix)
Simple syrup (see below)

Place ice in blender jar. Add orange juice and pudding mix, and fill to 24-ounce mark (on the blender jar) with Simple Syrup. Blend until mixed but ice crystals remain. Makes 1 quart.

MAKE SIMPLE SYRUP

2 cups slightly warm water
2 cups plus 3 tablespoons sugar

Mix water and sugar in quart jar. Let stand until liquid is clear, about 30 minutes, shaking occasionally. Store in refrigerator.

THE GROWN-UP ORANGE JULIUS

Okay, you knew my abstinence wasn't going to last, didn't you?

½ of a 6-ounce can of frozen orange juice concentrate, thawed, but not reconstituted
½ cup milk
½ cup vodka
¼ cup sugar (or slightly less)
½ teaspoon vanilla
6 or 7 ice cubes

Combine all ingredients except the ice in a blender container. Cover and blend until smooth, about 30 seconds. Add ice cubes, one at a time, and blend. Serve immediately. Serves 3.

The good news is since both of the above variations include fiber, they can be considered as health drinks.

▶ *Casseroles and One-Dish Meals*
(see also Pasta and individual ingredients)

NOODLES BAKED WITH HAM AND SOUR CREAM

Bring on the leftovers. This is a must-have recipe in every kitchen. You can substitute chicken or veal for the ham, or just about any other leftover, if you wish (I have even done it with leftover baked salmon). You can make it the night before and bake it the next day (let it set out to come to room temperature, or bake a little longer). It needs nothing but some good bread and a green salad to make a wonderful dinner.

½ pound of noodles, cooked according to package directions, and drained.
1½ cups sour cream
1½ cups cottage cheese
2 cups (more or less) of chopped cooked ham, see above
½ cup chopped bell pepper, green or red (if they bother you, leave them out; it's your tummy; or substitute some canned pimento for color)
½ cup chopped celery
¼ cup chopped onion
2 slightly beaten eggs
½ teaspoon salt
Fresh ground pepper
6 tablespoons of butter, melted

Butter a 3-quart casserole dish, and preheat the oven to 350°. Toss all ingredients in a large bowl until well mixed, and pour into the prepared casserole dish. Bake for 50-60 minutes, until bubbling hot. Serves 4 very generously.

HOMINY CHILI WITH BEANS

For your vegetarian friends, but don't let that put the rest of you off, it's delicious.

2 teaspoons vegetable oil
1 clove garlic, minced
4 teaspoons chili powder
1 teaspoon ground cumin
1 (15½ ounce) can white hominy, drained (or yellow if that's all you can find)
1 (15 ounce) can red beans, drained
1 (14½ ounce) can diced tomatoes, undrained
1 (14½ ounce) can stewed tomatoes, undrained and coarsely chopped
¼ cup sour cream (I use low fat, but be my guest)
¼ cup (1 ounce) shredded sharp cheddar cheese
4 teaspoon minced fresh cilantro

Heat oil in large saucepan over medium heat. Sauté garlic 1 minute. Stir in chili powder, cumin, hominy, red beans, and both cans tomatoes. Bring to boil, reduce heat and simmer, uncovered, 15 minutes. Spoon into 4 bowls; top each with 1 tablespoon sour cream, 1 tablespoon cheese and 1 teaspoon Cilantro.

BEEF ENCHILADA CASSEROLE

1 pound ground beef, cooked and drained (there's no reason you couldn't substitute ground chicken or turkey or make a vegetarian version by filling the enchiladas with ricotta cheese and cheddar, half and half)
2 cans (4 ounces each) chopped or diced green chilies, drained
1 can (4 ounces) chopped black olives, drained
3 cans (10 ounces each) enchilada sauce
2 cups grated cheddar or longhorn cheese
1 cup grated Monterey Jack cheese
1 package (20 ounces) flour tortillas

Heat oven to 350°, lightly grease a 9 x 13 baking dish. In a large bowl, combine meat, chilies and olives, mix well. Cover the bottom of the prepared dish with half the enchilada sauce. Combine cheeses and set aside. Top each tortilla with ¼ cup beef mix and ¼ cup cheese, roll up and place on enchilada sauce in dish, seam side down. Cover with remaining sauce, sprinkle remaining cheese on top, bake for 30-40 minutes. Serve topped with sour cream.

BAKED SPAGHETTI, WESTERN STYLE

This makes quite a bit. When making it for myself, I cut it in half. Everything else is easy to cut, except for the milk and the egg. To cut them in half, first combine the ⅓ cup milk and 1 egg, and beat. This measures about ½ cup and can easily be halved.

8 ounces Spaghetti, cooked al dente and drained
⅓ cup milk
1 egg
1 pound ground pork
1 medium onion, chopped
1 medium green pepper, chopped
1 fresh or canned jalapeño pepper, seeds and ribs removed, minced
1 tablespoon chili powder
½ teaspoon ground cumin
½ teaspoon dried oregano
½ teaspoon salt
1 16-ounce can tomato sauce
8 ounces shredded Monterey Jack cheese

Heat oven to 425°. Butter a 9 x 13 (or 3 quart) baking dish. Combine milk and egg and toss with cooked spaghetti. Spread in the baking dish. While the spaghetti is cooking, cook the pork, onion, green pepper and garlic in a large skillet about 6 minutes over medium heat, until pork is cooked through. Drain or spoon off excess fat. Add jalapeño, chili powder, cumin, oregano and salt and cook 2 minutes more. Add tomato sauce and cook 2 minutes. Spread meat sauce over pasta, sprinkle with cheese (can be assembled ahead and refrigerated). Bake in lower third of oven about 10 minutes or until it begins to bubble and cheese is melted. If made ahead, remove from refrigerator for 15 minutes or so before baking, then bake at 350° about 25 minutes. Let stand about 5 minutes.

CHICKEN OR TURKEY TETRAZZINI

A classic and savory way to use up leftovers, but it's good enough to justify buying a supermarket roasted chicken and using the meat from that. There are several steps but you can do all the dicing, measuring, grating, slicing, even sautéing the mushrooms, ahead of time, so you have only to make the sauce and cook the pasta when you're ready to fix dinner. I generally double this recipe, put it in two different baking dishes, cool one to room temperature and cover tightly with foil, and freeze-and I have a convenient dinner if company drops in or for one of those nights I don't feel like cooking.

2 cups (about) cooked chicken, skin removed and diced roughly
4 tablespoons butter
½ pound white mushrooms, trimmed and sliced ¼ inch thick
¼ cup all purpose flour
1½ cups milk
1½ cups chicken broth
¼ cup dry vermouth or dry sherry
1½ cups grated Parmesan cheese
¼ teaspoon dried thyme
½ pound linguine, broken in half
½ of a package (10 ounces) of frozen peas, about 1½ cups
Salt and pepper

Preheat oven to 400°. Salt a large pot of water and bring to a boil. Over high heat, melt 1 tablespoon of butter in a large saucepan, add mushrooms, season with salt and pepper and cook, stirring frequently, until tender, about 5 minutes. Transfer to a bowl, set aside. In the same saucepan, melt the remaining three tablespoons butter. Add flour and whisk for about 1 minute. Gradually whisk in the milk, broth and vermouth. Whisking constantly (if you got that flat bottomed whisk I recommend earlier, you don't have to do this constantly, just often) bring to a boil. Reduce to a simmer and add 1 cup of the Parmesan, the thyme, and salt and pepper to taste. Keep warm, stirring frequently.

Meanwhile, cook the pasta in the boiling water, stirring from time to time, for 2 minutes less than called for on the package for al dente. Drain, return the pasta to the pot off heat. Add the sauce, the chicken, peas and mushrooms and toss well. Pour into a shallow 2 quart baking dish and top with the remaining cheese. Bake about 30 minutes, or until the top is nicely browned. My oven is a bit slow, so

I sometimes crank up the heat the last 5 or 10 minutes, to get the top brown.

Or you can freeze it up to 3 months. To bake from frozen, leave covered with foil and bake at 400° for 2 hours. Uncover and bake about 20 minutes more, until top is nicely browned. Or, thaw first overnight in the refrigerator and bake, with the foil on, at 400° until warmed through, about 30 minutes, then uncover and bake about 20 minutes more to brown.

MEAT AND NOODLES

I'm almost embarrassed to include this here, but it is so easy, and so tasty, that I felt I had to share it. This is the dish for that evening when you know you must eat, and just haven't the energy to start cooking. Even take out isn't much quicker or simpler.

¾ to 1 pound ground meat-beef, lamb, pork or turkey
1 package (3 ounces) instant ramen noodles (select flavor to complement meat)
1 cup frozen vegetable mix (or, your choice of fresh vegetables-baby
carrots, broccoli, corn, *etc.*—see instructions below)
¼ teaspoon (or a pinch) ground ginger
2 tablespoons (more or less) thinly sliced green onions
1 cup stock (or hot water and bouillon) to match the meat and ramen
flavor (beef stock for beef ramen, etc.)

In skillet (preferably non-stick) brown meat over medium heat, 10-12 minutes, breaking it up with fork or spoon, until no longer pink. Remove meat from skillet with slotted spoon; pour off any drippings. Sprinkle the meat with the seasoning packet from ramen noodles and stir.

If you are using fresh vegetables: In same skillet, combine stock, and vegetables and simmer 2-3 minutes, depending on the vegetables, until vegetables are nearly done; Then add the noodles and ginger; bring to a boil, reduce heat, cover and simmer 3 minutes or until noodles are tender, stirring occasionally. Return meat to skillet, add green onions and stir just to reheat the meat—or:

If you are using frozen vegetables: In the same skillet, combine the vegetables with the stock, the noodles and ginger. Bring to boil, reduce heat. Cover. Simmer 3 minutes or until noodles are tender, stirring occasionally. Return meat to skillet, add green onions, stir just to reheat meat.

MEXICAN CASSEROLE

½ cups crushed tortilla chips
1 pound shredded cooked chicken meat (or substitute ground beef, cooked)
1 can (15½ ounces) garbanzos, drained
1 can (15½ ounces) kidney beans, drained
1 can (15½ ounces) corn kernels, drained
1 (8-ounce) can tomato sauce
1 cup prepared salsa
1 cup chopped red onion
1 green pepper cut in ¼ inch dice
¼ cup chopped cilantro leaves
1 tablespoon minced garlic
Salt and pepper to taste
6 ounces grated Monterey Jack
6 ounces grated sharp Cheddar
Garnishes: 2 cups diced (¼ inch) ripe tomatoes. 1 cup sour cream, ½ cup chopped fresh cilantro leaves

Heat oven to 350°. Grease 13 x 9 baking dish, then scatter crushed tortilla chips on bottom. Combine all the ingredients but the cheeses and garnishes. Place half in baking dish over the chips. Combine the two cheeses, sprinkle half on top; cover with remaining chicken mix, then remaining cheese. Bake for 30 minutes. Let stand for 5 minutes. Serve garnishes on the side.

MACARONI CHILI

This is perfect cold weather food, or for a Super Bowl party. It is more a Midwestern style chili than Texas or West Coast—i.e., more like a thick soup. It begs for a salad and lots of good bread to sop things up—it is not an elegant dish!

2 pounds ground beef
2 tablespoons olive or salad oil (if the meat looks fatty, 1 tablespoon will do)
1 can (28 ounces) tomatoes
1 quart tomato juice
2 cups chopped onion
3 cloves garlic, minced (or use a garlic press)
3 teaspoons salt

2 tablespoons chili powder
½ teaspoon cumin
½ teaspoon oregano
½ teaspoon black pepper, preferably fresh ground
1 bay leaf
1 can (15 ounces) red kidney beans
1 cup chopped sweet pickles (or mix sweet and dill)
2 cups elbow macaroni (8 ounces)

In large Dutch oven, brown beef in oil, stirring frequently. Add onions and garlic, sauté briefly, stirring. Add tomatoes, tomato juice, salt and seasonings. Simmer, covered, 1 hour. Let sit for a few minutes and skim off excess fat. Taste for seasoning, add more salt if necessary. I often goose up the chili powder, etc. Depends on how you like it.

(Note: this can be cooked as much as a day ahead to this point and refrigerated, which makes it easier to take off the fat. In either case, I reheat before preceding, then:)

Add kidney beans, cook 30 minutes. Meanwhile, bring a large pot of water (3 quarts more or less) to a boil and cook macaroni until tender, and drain. Add the macaroni and the pickles to chili just before serving, and remove the bay leave to be safe.

▶ *Pastas and Pasta Sauces*

SIMPLE TOMATO SAUCE

This is an excellent basic tomato sauce, which can be varied in many ways and used with all sorts of things: pasta or rice, of course, but with vegetables, too, and with lobster, shrimp or crab. With the seafood, you could add some sautéed bell pepper and some onion, and a bit of Tabasco, and you'd have a reasonable imitation of a **Creole sauce***. You can add some meat stock, mushroom stock, or sautéed mushrooms to the basic sauce, too. It is super with some Italian sausages poached in white wine, drained and smothered with the tomato sauce.*

Scald 3 pounds (more or less) tomatoes by pouring boiling water over them. Let sit for one minute, pour off water, dump tomatoes in ice water to stop the cooking. Peel them, halve them, and squeeze out seeds and juice (this is best over the sink or I like to do it right over the garbage can; the juice has a tendency to squirt all over the place), and chop coarsely (in French cooking, this is now a concassée of tomatoes). Melt 3 tablespoons butter and 3 tablespoons olive oil in a large saucepan; add the tomatoes, and heat to simmer over medium or medium low heat. Add 1 clove garlic, peeled but left whole, or more if you want, and some basil leaves, salt and pepper. If the tomatoes are very acid, add ¼ teaspoon sugar. Simmer gently for 45 minutes to 1 hour. Discard the garlic clove. If you want a thicker sauce, or if your tomatoes didn't have a lot of flavor, you can add some tomato paste.

BURNT BURST TOMATO SAUCE

This is a good basic sauce, too, as easy as any I know, and I like it with shrimp or chicken or over vegetables, as well as on pasta or polenta.

Preheat the broiler. Dump 1-2 pints of cherry tomatoes onto a rimmed baking sheet or broiler proof pan, pour ¼ cup or more of olive oil on them and toss to coat. Salt and pepper generously, toss them with 1 minced garlic clove and season aggressively with some dried thyme or oregano, or substitute basil, or any combination thereof. Put the baking dish as close as you can to your broiler element and cook 8-12 minutes, or until they have begun to release their juices and a few have charred slightly. You can use this at once, or hold at room temperature and reheat briefly if you want it hot. I like to stir this about and put it under the broiler again for more charring, but that is optional. Yummy!

PENNE ALL'ARRABBIATA

For a vegetarian version, just omit the sausage.

2 Italian sausages, mild or hot (or 1 of each)
3 medium cloves garlic
2 tablespoons tomato paste
1 (28-ounce) can whole tomatoes in juice, chopped
1 bay leaf
2 tablespoons chopped parsley (more or less)
2 tablespoons chopped basil (more or less)
½ teaspoon crushed red pepper flakes
¼ cup white wine
1 teaspoon salt
1 pound penne rigate, cooked per package directions
Freshly grated Parmesan or Asiago cheese

Remove sausage from casing and brown in 1 tablespoon oil in a 3-quart saucepan over medium heat, breaking the meat up as it cooks; or, brown the ground beef.

Chop 1 clove of the garlic and add to the saucepan, cook for 30 seconds.

Add tomato paste and cook, stirring for 2 minutes; add tomatoes and their juice and bay leaf, simmer for 30 minutes, uncovered.

While the sauce simmers, heat the water for the pasta, and thinly slice the 2 garlic cloves remaining. Heat 1 tablespoon oil in a 12-inch skillet over medium heat. Add garlic and cook 30 seconds, until just starting to turn pale gold

Add parsley, basil and crushed pepper to the skillet, cook 30 seconds. Add wine and boil 30 seconds. Stir into the tomato mixture, add salt and simmer 4-5 minutes. Set aside to keep warm while you cook the pasta.

In a large bowl, toss the hot pasta with the sauce, drizzle with 1 tablespoon oil and serve with cheese.

Or, combine pasta and sauce, pour into a casserole dish, top with the cheese, and bake in a 350° oven for 5-10 minutes, until cheese browns.

If desired, garnish with additional basil or parsley leaves. 4 servings.

Note: this is certainly better if you follow the steps above, but if you are short of time or patience, just add all the garlic to the meat in the first step, and after the 30 minutes of simmering, simply add the parsley, basil, crushed pepper, and wine to the sauce and cook for another 4-5 minutes. It will still be delicious, and I won't tell anybody you cheated. Promise.

PASTA PUTTANESCA

This recipe comes from Joseph de Marco, who says of it: "This is probably my favorite pasta sauce (until I change my mind and move on to someone...I mean, something else).

"Probably one of the reasons it's a favorite is because of the name—puttanesca—in the style of the whore. Who doesn't have a soft spot for a brazen hustler? Named after those women in Naples who brave dark nights and even darker streets, I like to apply it to both the male and female variety. It is said that the prostitutes would set out a bowl of pasta drenched in this sauce so that its aroma would attract clients. Others say it's because they had to cook meals quickly from ingredients at hand to give them more time to see clients. Who knows? Whatever the case, they came up with one hell of a sauce.

"I can't remember the first time I had this sauce but I do recall it was the name that attracted me before anything else. Then when I saw what the ingredients were, I knew I'd love it. A heady mix of anchovies (now stop that complaining, they melt into the sauce and give it a mysterious flavor that really makes this whore of a mix what it is), capers, olives, spices, and a rich tomato sauce. What's not to like? It's actually a classy piece of culinary work.

"This is a rich, tangy, salty sauce—it's supposed to be that way. Just like the people it's named after. It's an in-your-face experience, which you won't soon forget. Each of the ingredients, strong and flavorful on their own, create a wholly different taste once blended together. The anchovies will melt and even those people who claim

not to like them will savor the flavor they create in concert with everything else. The capers and olives will give this sauce a unique taste that you can't help but love.

"Just remember to use the best, freshest ingredients you can find—good olive oil is worth whatever you have to pay for it. Good kalamata olives along with those wrinkled cured olives will make your guests swoon."

2 tablespoons extra virgin olive oil (or more depending on the amount you want to make)

6 cloves of fresh garlic chopped (more if you like a sauce with hearty flavor)

1 tin of flat anchovies minced

1 teaspoon good crushed red pepper (more if you really want some bite)

20 kalamata olives

10-20 cured black olives (the wrinkled salty kind)

3 tablespoons capers (and a little of the juice from the bottle if you like)

2-3 tablespoons tomato paste

1 (32 ounce) can crushed tomatoes

1-2 (15-ounce) can(s) diced tomatoes or tomatoes or tomato sauce

¼ cup or more chopped flat leaf parsley

¼ cup or more basil

1-2 pounds spaghetti (cooked al dente)

Make your soffritto by placing the olive oil in a pot large enough to accommodate all the ingredients. Sauté the garlic until it is just beginning to turn a slight golden color, then toss in the anchovies and red pepper. Don't let it sauté too long—just two or three minutes or less. Stir it around and watch the anchovies begin to dissolve.

Now get the tomato paste and the smaller can of diced tomatoes or tomato sauce into the mix. Stir it up, mixing the paste and what's already in the pot thoroughly.

Once that's done, add the crushed tomatoes, the olives, parsley, basil, and let them cook together.

Some people allow it to cook down to a thicker consistency, some don't go quite that far. It's up to you.

At the same time boil a big pot of water for the pasta. And cook it until al dente (keep trying it to be sure). Remember that pasta keeps cooking even after you remove it from the water, so pull it out of the drink even before you think it's ready.

The pasta type is up to you—originally spaghetti was the pasta of choice but now you can find this wonderful sugo draped over almost any pasta; there's the alliterative penne puttanesca to be found at lots of restaurants, and there are others. I don't think I'll break any rules by saying that it's the sauce that makes the pasta in this case. As for other sauces, sometimes the pasta does make a difference. But, hey, this is the Whore's sauce and it'll deal with any pasta that comes along and pays its way.

Make sure you get some nice, crusty Italian bread for sopping up the sauce.

You can pass around cheese (grated sharp hard cheese)—but I like the sauce just the way it is. Spicy, salty, and brazen, this is an aptly named sauce.

A nice merlot, red Zinfandel, or a great Shiraz will go nicely with this dish.

*Joseph R. G. de Marco is a native Philadelphian who now divides his time between Philadelphia and Montréal. He has been editor of numerous publications (*The Weekly Gayzette *and* New Gay Life*) and has written extensively for the gay/lesbian press. His 1983 article "Gay Racism" was awarded the prize for excellence in feature writing by the Gay Press Association. His fiction and non-fiction have appeared in many anthologies: the_*Quickies *series (*Arsenal Pulp Press),* Men Seeking Men *(Painted Leaf Press),* Charmed Lives *(Lethe)* Gay Life *(Doubleday),* Paws and Reflect *(Alyson)* Hey Paisan! *(Guernica),* The International Encyclopedia of Marriage and Family *(Macmillan) and the* Encyclopedia of Men and Masculinites *(ABC CLIO) among others. He is most interested in writing mysteries but werewolves and vampires also inhabit his fiction. He is currently the editor of* Mysterical-E *(*www.mystericale.com*), and his website is* www.josephdemarco.com

RICK'S PICCHI PACCHI (PASTA WITH RAW SAUCE)

Here is another recipe from the Master of the Macabre, Rick R. Reed, which he tells me was a favorite summer weather recipe when he was growing up in his Sicilian family's un-airconditioned house—but, really, there are some things I could eat any time of year.

6 red, ripe plum tomatoes, peeled, seeded, and diced
10 fresh basil leaves, cut into a chiffonade (*don't get excited, dear, just slice them across in little ribbons—VJB*)

Red chili pepper flakes, to taste
4 garlic cloves, minced
¼-½ cup extra virgin olive oil (the very best, please)
1 tablespoon red wine vinegar
¼ pound aged Asiago, grated
1 pound pasta.

Combine the first six ingredients and let sit for an hour or so (do not refrigerate! It is a sacrilege to refrigerate tomatoes; they lose all their flavor). Boil the pasta in salted water until al dente—check the timing directions on the package. Toss with the sauce and serve with grated cheese.

PETE'S RED GRAVY

There are two distinct schools of Italian cooking; the first is authentically Italian, the second is New York/New Jersey Italian American (think The Godfather*), and while they have their similarities, they are also different. You would probably never find a sauce in Italy like this one. It is heavy and inelegant, but it was for many generations a staple of Italian cooking in the immigrant ghettoes of cities like New York City, and in countless "Italian" restaurants in virtually every American city of any size. It is also delicious. It was called "gravy" and was a Sunday night staple, with or without the meatballs that follow. This recipe came from an old friend, Pete Tombrello, who grew up in Brooklyn and who prepared just this sauce every weekend.*

Sauté 1 large onion, chopped, with 5 cloves of chopped garlic. Add 2 large (28-ounce) cans of crushed tomatoes, preferably with basil added, and 2 cans of water, and 1 small can tomato paste, and 1 can water. Season with a bay leaf, and about 1 tablespoon each of dried basil and oregano. Bring to a simmer, and simmer about ½ hour, stirring occasionally. Add meatballs (recipe follows) and simmer 1-1½ hours, till thickened, stirring often to make sure it doesn't stick to the bottom and burn. If it gets too thick, add a little more water. You can also add Italian sausages, sweet, hot, or mixed. Drop the sausages first in boiling water and simmer 5 minutes to remove some of the fat. Rinse in cold water, then add with the meatballs (below) to the gravy. Also, you can cook some peeled hard-boiled eggs in the gravy for the last 20-30 minutes or so, making sure they remain covered by the sauce or they will turn to rubber. This was intended to be a substantial Sunday night "supper."

PETE'S MEATBALLS

1½ pounds ground beef
2 cloves garlic, chopped
½ cup dry breadcrumbs, the seasoned ones—Progresso or Contadina
2 eggs
¼ cup grated Parmesan—don't use that stuff in the green cans, get
    some real cheese from a good deli.
Chopped parsley—about 1 tablespoon or to taste (the first time you
    make this, use 1 tablespoon; afterward, you will know whether
    you want more or less)
Fennel seeds—about 1 tablespoon or to taste (see above)
Salt and Pepper

Combine all, shape into meatballs about 1½ inches-2 inches round.
Cook in the gravy as directed above. You can make these ahead and
freeze them uncooked. You can also sauté them in a bit of olive oil
in a skillet, stirring them around gently as they cook to brown all
over. Sautéed, you can make yourself a fabulous sub on an Italian
roll with lots of that red gravy and some Parmesan. Invite me over.

SPAGHETTI ALLA CARBONARA

*This sounds more difficult than it is, but you should read through the
recipe a time or two to get the steps set in your mind, as when you
go to finish the dish, you will want to do everything quickly, and I
suggest a dress rehearsal before you fix it for company. After a time
or two, though, you will find it is mostly automatic.*

4 tablespoons soft butter
2 whole eggs
2 egg yolks
1 cup grated Parmesan, preferably freshly grated
1 pound spaghetti or linguine
8 slices bacon, or ideally 4 bacon and 4 pancetta, cut crosswise into
    4-inch pieces (Pancetta is an Italian bacon found in delis and spe-
    cialty stores)
1 teaspoon dried red pepper flakes, or a pinch ground red pepper
    (both optional)
½ cup heavy cream
Fresh ground black pepper

1 cup frozen green peas (also optional; some purists scream at the suggestion, but Marcella Hazen suggested it)

Beat the eggs and egg yolks with a fork till well blended, then stir in ½ cup of the cheese. Set aside.

Heat a large ovenproof serving bowl in a 200° oven, or fill with hot water. Bring a pot of salted water to full boil and while it is heating, fry the bacon in a large skillet over moderate heat, until crisp.

When the water is at a full boil, add spaghetti, stirring briefly to be sure strands do not stick together. Cook over high heat 7-12 minutes, or until al dente.

Pour off about half the bacon fat and stir the cream and red pepper into the pan. Bring to a simmer and keep warm until the spaghetti is done.

When spaghetti is done, drain thoroughly in a large colander, lifting strands with two forks to be sure all the water runs off. Transfer the spaghetti to the heated serving bowl (if you've used hot water, but sure to empty and dry the bowl well, but quickly so the bowl stays warm.) Stir in the butter, tossing and turning to be sure every strand is coated. Then stir in the hot bacon and cream mixture, and finally the beaten eggs and cheese, mixing everything thoroughly. The heat of the pasta and cream should cook the eggs on contact. If not, keep tossing and stirring till it does. Taste and season with salt and fresh ground black pepper. Serve at once with the remaining ½ cup grated cheese passed at the table.

▶ *Eggs and Brunch Dishes*
(see also Casseroles)

FLORENTINE CREPE CUPS

These are a terrific and substantial finger food for a party, and fine as a light luncheon dish or an appetizer as well. They can be served hot out of the oven, or at room temperature, or made the day ahead and reheated for about 20 minutes in a low (250°) oven, or frozen and reheated later. Some supermarkets sell already made crepes, but after a couple of practice tries, they're really easy to do, can be done ahead and frozen, and are great to have on hand for all kinds of luncheon dishes, desserts, etc. Once you have gotten the knack, you will be glad to have this in your repertoire, and it is fun to show off to a non-cook watching you in the kitchen—you will feel just like Julia Child.

For the **crepes:**
3 slightly beaten eggs
⅔ cup flour
½ teaspoon salt
1 cup milk

For the **filling**:
1½ cups (6 ounces) grated sharp cheddar cheese
3 tablespoons flour
3 eggs, slightly beaten
⅔ cup mayonnaise
10-ounce package frozen chopped spinach, thawed and drained
½ cup sliced mushrooms, about 4 ounces (bottled ones, well drained, are okay)
6 bacon slices cut into bits, cooked crisp and drained.
2 extra bacon slices, cut in ½-inch pieces and sautéed, for garnish, optional (allow to curl in the pan)
½ teaspoon salt

72

⅛ teaspoon freshly ground black pepper.

Make the crepes:
    Combine all ingredients, let stand for 30 minutes. Heat crepe pan or 8 inch skillet, preferably non-stick) over medium high heat, grease lightly, and pour about 2 tablespoons batter into pan, *quickly* swirling it around to cover bottom of pan, cook just on one side until lightly browned, about 1 minute. Lift out with your fingers to a warm plate, and repeat. Makes 12 crepes.

For the filling:
    Combine cheese and flour, toss together, then add all the remaining ingredients except the optional bacon garnish and mix well. Butter 12 muffin cups and fit one crepe down into each to make a free-form cup. Fill with the cheese mixture and bake in a preheated 350° oven for 40 minutes, or until set. Garnish with additional bacon curls if desired. 2 cups equals one serving for brunch, or one cup for an appetizer.

TOAD IN THE HOLE

This is fun, and although your British friends will wonder why you bothered, most Americans will not have had it. The bonus is, it's quite good.

8 ounces pork sausage breakfast links (about 16 sausages)
1 tablespoon vegetable oil
1¼ cups milk
4 large eggs
Scant ½ teaspoon salt
1½ cup flour

Heat oven to 450°. Place sausages in baking dish about 9 inches square by 3 deep. Rub sausages with oil and oil bottom and sides of pan as well. Bake until lightly browned, about 15 minutes. Meanwhile, whisk milk, eggs and salt, set aside. When sausages are nearly ready, add flour to milk and mix until smooth. Transfer sausages to a plate, set aside. Pour just enough batter into hot pan to cover bottom. Return to oven and bake until batter is set, about 5 minutes. Arrange sausages evenly across top of batter and quickly pour in rest of batter. Return to oven and bake until batter billows up around sausages and has a crusty top, about 25 minutes. Cut into squares and serve immediately, because it will sink as it cools.

EGGS CHIMAY

This is a great brunch dish and has the added advantage that you can completely assemble it ahead and just pop it under the broiler or into a 400°-degree oven at the last minute, just to warm through and brown. This makes 2 servings, but it doesn't require a Ph.D. to multiply it for more.

Halve lengthwise 2 hard-boiled eggs. Remove yolks and break them up well with a fork. Mix with roughly two tablespoons finely chopped and cooked mushrooms, 3 tablespoons soft butter, 1 tablespoon Mornay sauce (see Sauces) and a dash of cayenne. Fill reserved whites with mixture, mounding it high. Spread a layer of Mornay sauce in gratin dish, arrange eggs face down in the sauce and coat with more of the sauce, being sure to cover eggs entirely or they will get rubbery. Sprinkle with grated Parmesan and lightly brown sauce under a broiler or in hot oven, to heat through.

WELSH RABBIT

*This is sometimes incorrectly called Welsh rarebit. Please have the good taste not to perpetuate the mistake. I have included this "recipe"—which is largely a matter of using convenience foods-for the benefit of those of you who feel you really cannot cook. You can make a very nice brunch dish of this. It will serve 4 nicely, and you can simply multiply it for more, and with the additional of some fruit, perhaps a fresh fruit mélange from your supermarket salad bar, and a bit of wine or juice, you will have a complete meal. As a suggestion, in place of the salad bar, try **Grapefruit with Campari**, which requires nothing more than halving and sectioning grapefruits, ideally the pink or red ones, and sprinkling each half with a teaspoon or so of Campari or, lacking that, sweet vermouth Let them sit half an hour or so. Serve them while the other things are cooking.*

2 packages Stouffers frozen Welsh Rarebit (sic), thawed
1 tablespoon Worcestershire sauce or, if you have a can open, dark
    beer
½ teaspoon Dijon mustard, optional
4 slices of bread, toasted (or you can use English muffins)
8 slices of bacon cut in half lengthwise
3-4 large ripe tomatoes, cut into slices (you will need 16 slices, but
    if they are large, you can cut some of them in two)

Cook the bacon. I find the easiest way to do this is to put it in a baking pan—I line mine with foil to ease cleanup—and bake at 350° for 20-30 minutes, until brown and crisp, turning once. Depending on the bacon, you might want to drain the fat when you turn it over, but don't get too prissy about this, a little fat in the pan helps make it crispier. Meanwhile, heat the cheese rarebit (sic) with the mustard and the beer or the Worcestershire sauce in the top of a double boiler. If you don't have one of those, put them in a saucepan or heatproof bowl and set that in a pan of simmering water. In either case, stir occasionally. When the bacon and the sauce are done, keep warm and toast the bread and cut each slice in 4 triangles. Arrange 4 pieces on each plate, top each piece with a slice of tomato, then a slice of bacon, and finally spoon the cheese sauce over all, and serve while still hot. Or put the bacon on top last, if you want it crispier.

LEMON RICOTTA HOT CAKES

These are positively addictive. I recommend making them small, as they are a bit fragile and can break when you turn them. However, they are also forgiving, and I just push them back together in the pan. These really beg for some fresh raspberries, or at least the very best jam, the imported stuff with the liqueur in it.

6 large eggs, separated
1½ cups whole-milk ricotta cheese
1 stick unsalted butter, melted and cooled
½ teaspoon pure vanilla extract (see my introductory notes)
½ cup all purpose flour
¼ cup sugar
½ teaspoon salt
2 tablespoons grated lemon zest (about 2 lemons)
Powdered sugar for dusting (optional, but this is hardly the time to
    think about your waistline, dearie)

Beat together ricotta, butter, egg yolks, and set aside. Heat griddle or a large non-stick skillet. Stir together flour, sugar, salt and lemon zest. Whip egg whites until they hold firm, glossy peaks. With rubber spatula, stir dry ingredients gently into the ricotta mixture. Stir a spoonful of the whipped egg whites into the batter, then gently fold in the rest of the egg whites. Grease the heated griddle, if necessary. Drop batter onto griddle, a tablespoon or two at a time. Cook until golden on the bottom and the top shows a bubble or two. Turn carefully and cook until undersides are light brown. Keep warm, covered, in a 200°-degree oven while you cook the remaining batter. Dust generously with powdered sugar to serve. (If you like, brush the cakes with a little melted butter before putting them in the warming oven. Yes, it adds calories and cholesterol. Yes, they are even more delicious. I have trouble enough with my own conscience. I can't handle yours.)

GRANDMA MUSTON'S FLANNEL CAKES

This recipe comes from Ken Beemer, who lives in Norfolk, Virginia, and is an avid reader, and a pipe organ technician (no, gang, I am not going anywhere near that! VJB).

2 cups sifted flour
1 teaspoon salt
3 teaspoons baking powder
2 eggs, separated
2 cups milk
2 tablespoons melted shortening (or oil)

Sift flour, salt and baking powder together. Beat egg yolks and add milk and oil, combine. Add dry ingredients and blend well. Beat egg whites until stiff and glossy and gently fold into batter. Cook on a hot griddle like ordinary pancakes.

HARD-BOILED EGGS

There are so many different theories on how to hard boil eggs. Julia once did an entire show on HB eggs, as she dubbed them, the goal being to show you perfect boiled eggs without that ugly green ring around the yolk. At the end of the show, she cracked an egg, and there it was, the great green ring. My own take on the matter is that you don't want to boil them at all; you want the water just barely simmering. I prick one end of each egg with a safety pin, salt the water heavily (which makes them easier to peel afterward), bring the water to the merest shiver and lower the eggs gently into the water. I set the timer for 14 minutes, or 15 if the eggs have just come from the refrigerator, but a minute or two before that, I lift one or two out of the water with a slotted spoon. If the shell dries off completely in a twinkling, they are done. I pour off the hot water and put the eggs in cold water to stop the cooking. The easiest way to peel them is under cold running water; then dry them gently on paper towels.

IMPOSSIBLE SCRAMBLED EGGS

This comes from a very popular diner in Sydney famous for their scrambled eggs, and I can see why. I have to confess, I chickened out and reduced the cream to ¼ cup, and that was still unbelievably rich, but delicious. One day I may get up the courage to go all the way. Maybe even with these eggs. This is one serving.

¼ ounce butter (a mere sliver)
2 eggs
½ cup heavy cream
Pinch of salt

Whisk eggs, cream, and salt together. Melt the butter in a nonstick pan over high heat, pour in the eggs and—this takes nerve—do nothing for 20 seconds. Then with a wooden spoon or heatproof spatula, stir slowly, folding the rim of the mixture toward the center—do not churn away like a cement mixer. Pause for another 20 seconds, then repeat the gentle stirring and folding process. At this point, the recipe says to take the pan from the heat and let the residual heat complete the cooking, before giving the eggs one last swirl. But that left them a bit soft for me and I gave them a third 20-second cooking before taking from the heat. Yes, they are wonderful. And that funny crackling noise is your arteries hardening.

VICTOR'S BRUNCH CASSEROLE

The result of experimenting with 3 or 4 similar recipes—this is the version I like best. The beauty of this is you do it the night before and just have to fling it in the oven in the morning—that way you've got more time for a Bloody Mary.

8-10 slices white bread (preferably day-old Italian or French, but don't get too princess-y about this, it's just bread.)
1 pound pork sausage
2 cups cooked cubed chicken
1 cup diced celery
2 cups shredded cheddar (separated, 1¾ cups and ¼ cup)
3 eggs, slightly beaten
1 cup mayonnaise
1½ cups milk
½ cup half and half

½ teaspoon poultry seasoning
Salt and pepper to taste

Remove and cube the crusts from the bread slices. Butter the slices and cut into quarters. Brown and drain the sausage and spread in the bottom of a casserole. Combine crust *cubes* (not the slices) with the chicken, celery and 1¾ cups of shredded cheddar; pour over the top of the sausage. Top with the buttered bread slices to more or less cover all.

Combine the eggs, mayonnaise, milk, half and half, poultry seasoning, salt, and pepper, and pour egg mixture over chicken/bread mix. Sprinkle with ¼ cup shredded cheddar. Refrigerate overnight.

In the morning, bake uncovered at 350° for 45 minutes or until nicely browned.

SPINACH QUICHE

1 package Stouffers frozen Spinach soufflé, defrosted
Pastry for 1 single crust pie
¾-1 cup shredded Swiss cheese, divided (see below) about 3 ounces
6 rashers bacon, cut into bits and partially cooked
¼ cup sour cream
3 eggs, lightly beaten
2 tablespoons chopped green onion (2-3 scallions, depending on size)
1 tablespoon all purpose flour
Pinch of black pepper
Pinch of nutmeg

Preheat oven to 375°. Spray pie pan or quiche pan with non-stick spray. Put piecrust in pan, crimp edges. Scatter partially cooked bacon on bottom of crust Combine defrosted soufflé, ½ cup cheese, sour cream, eggs, green onion, flour, pepper and nutmeg in bowl. Spoon into pie shell. Sprinkle remaining cheese on top.

Cover edges of crust with foil. Bake for 15 minutes; remove foil, bake for 15-20 minutes more until crust and filling are well brown. Cool on rack 5 minutes before serving. If desired, garnish with sliced rings of the green parts of scallion and/or diced pimento or diced tomato.

EASY CHEESE SOUFFLÉ

This is another recipe for those who think they can't cook. You can even reheat the leftovers the next day. It is practically indestructible, though it lacks the elegant lightness of the more traditional soufflé.

Preheat oven to 300°. In 1-quart saucepan, combine 1 can Cream of Cheddar Soup, 1 cup shredded Cheddar Cheese, and a dash of cayenne pepper. Stir occasionally over low heat until cheese melts and remove from heat.

Separate 6 eggs. Beat whites with a dash of Cream of Tarter at high speed until stiff peaks form. In separate bowl, beat egg yolks until thick and lemon colored. Gradually stir egg yolks into the soup mixture, and fold in whites. Pour into ungreased 2-quart casserole or soufflé dish. Bake 1 hour or until lightly browned. Makes 6 servings.

This works well with different flavor combinations: Cream of Asparagus soup with Swiss cheese and ⅛ teaspoon ground nutmeg, for instance; or tomato soup with American cheese and ¼ teaspoon marjoram leaves, crushed; or Cream of Chicken with Jarslberg and 2 tablespoons chopped parsley.

A MAKE-AHEAD OMELET

Truth is, I have never been sure what to call this, since it isn't quite an omelet, and it isn't quite a soufflé, either, but it is their next door neighbor, and by any name, it is delicious, and amazingly versatile. The recipe that follows features mushrooms for the filling, but you can use almost anything that you have. It would be excellent with crab meat and frozen thawed artichokes, chopped, about 6 ounces altogether of the two; or spinach and crumbled bacon; leftover vegetables would be terrific as well, or some really good tomatoes, peeled, seeded, chopped, well drained and tossed with a few sun dried tomatoes. You can substitute other cheese, such as Parmesan or Romano, but not soft cheeses (Brie, e.g.), as this will change the moisture balance and the "loft." To serve a large number of people, double the recipe and bake in a 9 x 13 x 2 inch baking dish.

6 ounces finely chopped mushrooms, any mix (shitakes, white button, Portobello, chanterelle)
1 tablespoon finely chopped shallot, or substitute scallions, the white parts only
1 tablespoon olive oil

1 tablespoon flour
¼ cup heavy cream
½ cup Wondra flour, or substitute all-purpose
1 cup milk
3½ tablespoons unsalted butter
½ teaspoon salt
⅛ teaspoon freshly ground black pepper (or a generous pinch)
⅛ teaspoon grated nutmeg
4 eggs
4-5 ounces Gruyère cheese, grated coarsely, about 1 cup, plus another 2-3 tablespoons to sprinkle on top.

Generously butter the sides and bottom of a 9-inch square baking pan, preferably glass or ceramic and set aside. Place the oven rack in the upper one third of the oven and preheat the oven to 400°. (That is, if you are baking this at once. If you plan to make this ahead and bake it later, see notes below.)

Make the filling: in a small saucepan, sauté the mushrooms and shallots in the oil for 5 minutes, stirring frequently. Reduce the heat and sprinkle the flour over the mushrooms. Cook and stir for 1 minute. Remove the saucepan from the heat and stir in the cream. Return the pan to the heat and cook over medium heat, stirring, until thickened. Season with salt and pepper and set aside.

Make the cheese base: put the flour in a heavy bottom saucepan and whisk in the milk. Cook over medium high heat, stirring slowly and constantly, until it comes to a boil and thickens. Remove from the heat and beat in the butter, the seasonings and the eggs, one at a time. Then beat in the shredded cheese.

Spread half the cheese base in the bottom of the prepared pan, spoon the mushroom filling over the top, and cover with the remaining cheese mixture. Sprinkle additional grated cheese on top. Bake 25 minutes, until puffy and golden brown.

Alternatively, once you have assembled the omelet, you may cover it with Saran wrap and refrigerate it up to 2 days. To bake, preheat the oven to 400°, remove the Saran wrap, and bake for 30-40 minutes.

MR. AND MRS. MURPHY

Another dish that even a non-cook can do, and these can be made ahead—I have even made them and frozen them, wrapped tightly, and baked them later. They are awfully good with fresh asparagus in butter—if you sauté the lobster meat in butter, use that butter on *the asparagus; why waste the flavor? Serve with **baked cherry to-matoes**—roll them in some oil and bake them briefly with the potatoes, just to heat through.*

4 medium baking potatoes (Idahos)
6 ounces lobster meat (ideally, from your fishmonger or buy frozen tails, thaw, remove the meat from the shells and sauté as below)
½ cup butter
½ cup half and half
1 teaspoon salt
⅛ teaspoon cayenne pepper
4 teaspoons grated onion (use a box grater and the larger holes)
1 cup grated sharp cheddar cheese
½ teaspoon paprika

Set oven at 325°. Scrub potatoes well and dry thoroughly. Bake about 20 minutes; pierce the skin of each 2 or 3 times with a fork. Bake 40 minutes or until soft when pierced with fork. Pick over the lobster carefully to remove any cartilage. If you use frozen thawed lobster tails, cut into chunks. Sauté and toss the lobster meat for 2- 3 minutes in some hot butter, until opaque throughout. Drain and save the butter (see above). If you bought already cooked lobster meat, toss in the hot butter only for a minute. Cut baked potatoes in half lengthwise, scoop out potato, leaving enough "meat" on the skins to provide shells for stuffing. Whip the removed potato meat with an electric mixer with the butter, cream, salt, cayenne, onion and cheese. With fork or spoon, mix in lobster and refill shells. Sprinkle with paprika and reheat in a very hot oven, 450°, for about 15 minutes, until browned on top. If making ahead, wait to bake them when you're ready to serve.

ASPARAGUS TART

A fabulous luncheon or brunch dish. You can make puff pastry shells for dessert tarts the same way; if the dessert will not be baked again after filling, bake the shell a bit longer until nicely browned. This is particularly pretty if made with alternate stalks of white asparagus (well peeled) and green, but you must select green stalks of about the same thickness as the (peeled) white ones, so everything will cook in about the same time. I have made a less expensive but still tasty version with tiny broccoli and cauliflower florets.

1 sheet of Pepperidge Farm frozen puff pastry dough (from a 17.3-ounce package) thawed according to package directions.
1 cup (about) of Shredded Gruyère cheese, about 3 ounces
1 pound (about) of medium thick or thick asparagus spears
1 tablespoon olive oil
salt and freshly ground pepper
1-2 tablespoons freshly grated Parmesan cheese.

Preheat the oven to 400°. Cover a baking sheet with non-stick aluminum foil or parchment paper. Put the pastry dough on the sheet and, with the tip of a sharp knife, lightly score the dough on all four sides, about 1 inch in from the edge. Inside the markings, pierce the dough with the tines of a fork at ¼ inch intervals. This will be easier to understand if you read the instructions through and get a picture in your mind of where this is going. When you bake the pastry, the fork-pierced interior will remain more or less flat (you may have to re-pierce it again while it bakes, or immediately upon removing it from the oven, if it insists on rising) while the border will rise without restriction, forming the walls of your shell. Bake the shell about 15 minutes, until lightly golden. Don't let it get brown, as it will be baking some more when filled and you don't want it to burn.

Remove the shell from the oven and sprinkle the grated Gruyère cheese in the bottom. Trim the asparagus to fit inside the shell and place it snugly in rows, alternating tips and bottoms (if the spears are too short to reach across, just trim enough from another stalk and fill it with that). Brush the asparagus with the oil, sprinkle with salt and pepper, and sprinkle with the additional Parmesan. Return to the oven and bake about 20-30 minutes more, until the spears are tender. If the sides of the shell are getting too dark, cover the tops with strips of foil. Cut into quarters for a luncheon dish. Alternatively, to make finger foods for a party, cut the pastry sheet in half and make 2 narrower tarts, following the same instructions. As finger food, these will hold together better in smaller pieces and be easier to pick up. Serve warm or at room temperature. Puff pastry is better if baked and eaten the same day, but you can make the shells and freeze them unbaked (I like to have a few of these on hand) and let the shell sit out at room temperature for half an hour to thaw before proceeding with the cooking.

▶ *Poultry*

SORT OF JULIA'S CHICKEN SALAD

This is another dish that even the beginner can do that will impress your fussiest foodie friends. If you really are a beginner, buy a pre-cooked chicken from your market. If you live near a Costco, it's hard to beat their rotisserie chicken. If you want to do your own and can find an old stewing hen, this is the perfect time to roast one or better yet, "boil" it in barely simmering water with some aromatic vegetables. None of these measurements need be exact. This is my adaptation of Julia Child's recipe.

About 1 quart diced chicken meat, ideally light and dark combined
2-3 cups diced celery
½ cup finely minced shallots, or substitute scallions
⅓ cup chopped parsley, preferably the curly Italian kind
Salt and pepper
Juice from 1 whole lemon
4 or more tablespoons olive oil or grapeseed oil
½ cup to 1 cup walnuts pieces (or pecans or cashews or whatever
    you like)
About 1 cup of seedless grapes, halved (or use orange or tangerine
    segments, seeded; or diced apple)
2 cups or more of mayonnaise
Lettuce leaves or a chiffonade of lettuce—don't get nervous, a chif-
    fonade is just the whole head of lettuce sliced across to make lit-
    tle ribbons when it falls apart

Fold together the chicken, celery, scallions, parsley, about ½ tea-spoon of salt and several grinds of black pepper; toss with 2 table-spoons lemon juice and 2 of oil. Taste for seasoning, cover and let rest for at least 30 minutes in the refrigerator. When you are ready to assemble, drain off any accumulated juices and fold in nuts and fruit. Fold in mayonnaise. Put lettuce leaves on a platter, salt and pepper them, mound chicken salad on top, glaze the top with additional mayonnaise. Garnish as desired (I like cucumber slices)

CHICKEN CHASSEUR (HUNTER'S CHICKEN)

Yum. A fabulous winter dish to have in your repertory. This is hearty and wonderful, and sloppy (which reminds me of someone I once knew) and reheats nicely-which is more than I could say about that aforementioned individual.

6-8 chicken thighs, or mix thighs and drumsticks, or any combination you like. I use boneless skinless thighs and drumsticks with bone in, skin on, because it's just too much work to skin a drumstick, in my opinion, but be my guest.
Salt and pepper
2 tablespoons olive oil
2 tablespoons butter
2 cloves of garlic, chopped
6 portabella mushrooms (or mix portabellas and shitakes, or whatever you find at the market), caps only, roughly chopped
2 tablespoons flour (plus extra for dredging the chicken)
2 cups white wine or dry vermouth
2 cups chicken stock
1 28-ounce can diced tomatoes, with juice
2 tablespoons tomato paste
1 tablespoon chopped rosemary.

Heat the oven to 350°. Salt and pepper the chicken and dredge lightly in flour (that just means coat it; the easiest way is to put the flour in a bag, drop in the chicken and shake it heartily—I mean, the bag with the chicken). In a large heavy skillet, heat the oil over medium high heat until hot and add the butter. Brown the chicken until a toasty golden brown (not too dark), starting skin side down (if skin on) and don't crowd the pan. Brown the second side. As the pieces are browned, remove to an ovenproof casserole.

Cook the onion in the same pan, over medium heat, for about 10 minutes, stirring often, until the onion softens without browning. Add the garlic, mushrooms, salt and pepper, cook, stirring often, for about 5 minutes, add 2 tablespoons of flour, stir and continue cooking for about 2-3 minutes more.

Remove onion mushroom mixture to the casserole with the chicken and pour the wine into the skillet, bring to a boil, scraping the bottom of the pan to loosen any brown bits (this is called the "fond"). Pour into the casserole. Heat stock and add to the casserole. Heat the tomatoes and add to the casserole (I do all this in the microwave, or you can do it in the skillet. It's not necessary to heat these things separately, it's just my skillet wouldn't accommodate it all together and you want to have everything hot to start or it will take a long time to come to the simmer in the oven. Add the tomato paste and the rosemary to the casserole, and stir everything thoroughly. Cover the casserole (foil is okay) and bake for 15 minutes. Uncover, and bake 30 minutes longer or until the meat is falling off the bone tender. Serve this over penne or other pasta.

VICTOR'S BOSOMS

Properly, a breast has nipples, and since chickens do not, I prefer to call them bosoms. Besides, when you tell your guests what you are serving them, it is bound to disconcert them, and what is the point of having a party if you can't have some fun?

3 chicken bosoms, halved (6 pieces)
Pepper
6 bacon slices
6-8 slices dried beef
1 can cream of chicken soup
¾ cup sour cream
1½ ounces cream cheese
Hot rice or noodles

Pepper (do not salt) chicken; wrap each piece in 1 slice bacon. Place a layer of dried beef in the bottom of baking dish, arrange chicken on top. Combine soup, sour cream and cream cheese; pour over chicken. Cover tightly with foil. Bake at 350° for 1 hour; remove foil and let brown slightly. Serve on bed of hot rice or noodles

GARLIC CHICKEN

Don't get nervous about the large quantity of garlic. Cooked long and slowly like this, it loses its pungency and imparts, instead, a mellow, nutty flavor.

2-3 pound fryer cut into serving pieces
40 cloves of garlic, peeled
Grated zest of 1 lemon

Juice of 1 lemon
½ cup dry vermouth
¼ cup olive oil
4 ribs celery, thickly sliced on diagonal
2 tablespoons finely chopped parsley
2 teaspoons dried basil
1 teaspoon dried oregano
Pinch crushed red pepper flakes
Salt and pepper to taste

Preheat over 375°. Place chicken, skin up, in single layer in shallow baking pan. Combine garlic, wine, vermouth, oil, celery, parsley, basil oregano and pepper flakes in medium size bowl, mix thoroughly, Sprinkle over chicken, sprinkle zest over and around chicken, pour lemon juice over top, season with salt and pepper. Cover pan with foil, bake 40 minutes. Remove foil, bake 15 minutes or until chicken is tender.

DUSTIN'S RED CHICKEN CURRY

Dustin P. Roèbére, the naked story teller, sends this intriguing recipe, and says, "An excellent chef somewhere developed this great dish. The recipe was found as part of a Macintosh computer database (I think that qualifies as hidden treasure—VJB). No credit was mentioned. Perhaps it was cooked with several ingredients being added or deleted to make a different finished product at each meal. A wonderful recipe, one that you should definitely take the time to prepare, as the Red Curry Spice will tantalize your taste buds."

1 small yellow onion
½ red bell pepper
½ yellow bell pepper
1 small, ripe mango
1 teaspoon chopped garlic
1 cup boiled chicken, cut in ¾-inch chunks
1-2 tablespoons peanut oil
¼ cup water
¼ cup port wine
⅛ cup (2 tablespoons) dark rum
2 tablespoons rice wine vinegar
2 teaspoons or more of Red Curry Powder, recipe follows
Salt
Cooked rice

Peel the peppers, remove seeds and dice into ½ to ¾ inch pieces, and set aside. Peel and slice mango, being careful not to get too close to the seed, where the flesh is stringy. Dice that into ½ to ¾ inch chunks and set aside. Place a non-stick skillet on medium-high heat. Add oil. From this point on, stir frequently. Add red curry powder and stir well into the hot oil. This brings out the flavors in the spices. Immediately add onion and red and yellow peppers. As soon as the onions start to turn translucent, add the garlic and continue stirring about one minute. Add the rum, wine, water and vinegar. Add the mango and chicken last. Cook until liquid thickens. There should be enough sauce left to slightly moisten the rice. Salt to taste before serving. Adding salt before the liquid has reduced can fool you into over-salting. Serve over boiled white or brown rice.

Substitutions and hints: The mango must be completely ripe. If mango is not available, Bosc pears or Granny Smith apples both work well. In that case, the addition of several tablespoons of mango chutney is also nice. Chutney tends to be salty, so you may not need any salt. Other fresh peppers may be added or substituted. As many as seven different kinds have been used in one dish, including green, red and yellow bell peppers; green, red and white jalapeños; Anaheims, serranos, and banana peppers. Peeling the peppers is not absolutely necessary, but it enhances the digestibility and improves the overall texture of the dish. If the mango and port together are a bit sweet to your taste, try a dry (but not sour) wine, but nothing too obtrusive. Or, try brandy in place of both the wine and the rum. If you start with raw chicken, you might need to add some more water or chicken stock and give the chicken more time to cook. This might overcook the vegetables, so an alternative would be to add the chicken in just before the garlic. Other cooking oils may be substituted for peanut oil, but olive oil is a bit strong and may detract from the flavors of the spice. Red onions work well, as do shallots.

RED CURRY POWDER

Grind together:
2 teaspoons whole black peppercorns
6 whole cloves
4 teaspoons coriander seeds
1 whole nutmeg

Add ground spices:
¼ teaspoon allspice

2 teaspoons cardamom
½ teaspoon cayenne
¼ teaspoon cinnamon
⅛ teaspoon ginger
3 teaspoons Hungarian paprika
3 teaspoons pasilla chili powder
½ teaspoon turmeric
Other possible spices are cumin, fennel, black mustard seeds, and
  bay leaf

Use a coffee or spice grinder to grind the whole spices, then add the other spices and grind the entire mixture together for several seconds to blend well. The spices in the curry powder are based on personal taste and on what is available. This should just be a starting point for your own recipe. Instead of pasilla chili, try California or New Mexico chili powders. New Mexico tends to be hotter, so if you use that, you may want to decrease the cayenne. Inexpensive paprika may have no flavor at all, therefore the call for Hungarian paprika. Be careful about increasing the quantities of cinnamon, ginger or cloves. Any of them can easily become too dominant. The most interesting thing is when you cannot quite identify the individual spices.

TACO WINGS

2 pounds chicken wings, halved, and the wingtip discarded
1 package dry Taco seasoning
¼ cup cornmeal
¾ teaspoon salt
2 teaspoons parsley flakes, or fresh parsley chopped fine

Combine all in plastic bag. Shake wings a few at time in bag until coated. Place in single layer on greased shallow baking pans, bake at 350° for 20 minutes, turn and bake 10 minutes, until tender.

LORI'S INCREDIBLY TASTY SOY SAUCE CHICKEN WINGS

This is from Lori Lake, author of the critically acclaimed Snow Moon Rising *and many other novels and short stories. Lori says: "They are SO YUMMY! Diane and I have been making these for 25 years and we have them every year at the annual Superbowl party— which is less about football and more of an excuse for friends to come over and eat homemade Chinese foods!" (I would even sit through the football game for food like this, and the last time I actually sat through a football game, I was dating this quarterback and...oh, never mind, these things do get away from me. VJB).*

3-4 pounds chicken wings—if you get whole wings, cut off and discard the small meatless joint at the end
2 cups low-salt soy sauce (*Ohsawa Nama Shoyu Organic is best, if you can find it; if not, Kikkoman is very traditional; VJB*)
2 tablespoons olive oil
½ cup white wine (or water)
1 tablespoon sugar
1 teaspoon ground ginger
1 teaspoon garlic powder (or fresh crushed garlic if you prefer)
1 teaspoon onion powder (or fresh minced onion if you prefer)
¼ teaspoon black pepper (optional)
¼ teaspoon white pepper (optional)

Wash wings thoroughly. Place side by side in one huge cake pan. Combine remaining ingredients. To thoroughly mix the marinade, it works best to put everything into a sealable container and shake the hell out of it.

Pour the sauce over the wings. Cover with plastic wrap and marinate for 72 hours in the refrigerator If the liquid doesn't completely cover the wings, make sure you turn them over 2 or 3 times.

After marinating, preheat oven to 325°.

Lay out wings on a high-gloss or non-stick cookie sheet—they make quite a mess, so make sure it's an easy sheet to clean up (*Note: or line the sheet with Reynold's non stick aluminum foil. VJB*).

Bake 30 minutes, then turn. Bake 30 minutes more, then turn. Bake a final 30-40 minutes, until dark mahogany brown. Remove and serve with rice or other not-so-salty foods.

After baking, the wings can be stored in the refrigerator for up to 72 hours, or they can be wrapped in foil and frozen and removed at a later date and re-baked (in the foil) until heated through.

GARLIC LIME CHICKEN BREASTS

3 whole breasts with skin and bone, halved (6 pieces)
¼ cup rum
¾ cup hot water
3 limes, halved
6 tablespoons minced garlic

Hot pepper flakes
Salt

Wipe the chicken breasts with damp cloth. Set breasts in shallow baking dish skin side up and pour the hot water and the rum around them. Squeeze juice from one half of a lime over each breast, then scatter 1 tablespoon minced garlic over each breast. Sprinkle liberally with hot pepper and salt lightly. Bake in 350° oven for about 50 minutes, until fork tender.

EMILY'S HONEY PECAN CHICKEN

This is sinfully rich. From my niece, Emily Medearis, an avid reader

Marinate chicken breasts in buttermilk. Dredge with flour seasoned with salt and pepper. Optional: add cayenne and tarragon to the flour. Sauté until golden brown and cooked through. Meanwhile melt ½ cup butter and ½ cup honey; add ½ cup roasted chopped pecans. Pour over chicken and serve.

SLOW-ROASTED GARLIC AND LEMON CHICKEN

This gains flavor from the slow cooking. You can use all legs and thighs, or breasts, or a combination.

3-4 pounds chicken pieces
1 head garlic, separated into unpeeled cloves
2 lemons cut into eighths (more or less)
Small handful of fresh thyme, more or less as you like it, or use another herb
3 tablespoons olive oil
⅔ cup dry vermouth
Black pepper

Preheat oven to 300°. Put chicken, garlic, and lemon in roasting pan. Roughly pull the leaves off some of the thyme, saving some whole to strew over later. Add the oil to the pan and toss everything together (Sorry, but the best way to do this is with your hands, and wash them thoroughly afterward) and spread everything out, making sure the chicken pieces are all skin side up. Sprinkle with vermouth and fresh ground pepper. Cover *tightly* with foil and cook for 2 hours. Remove foil and turn oven up to 400°. Cook uncovered for

30-45 minutes, till the skin is golden brown and the lemons have begun to scorch a bit at the edges. Strew with remaining thyme and serve as soon as possible while the skin is still crisp.

THE DEVIL'S CHICKEN

This is probably not for the beginner. I wouldn't rank it terribly difficult, but there's a lot to do and I think when you're just beginning, simple is better.

1 chicken, spatchcocked (this just means take out the backbone and split the chicken, leaving the halves attached at the breast, and flatten it slightly. Your butcher will almost certainly do this for you, but all you really need is some sharp scissors and it's not that complicated. If you're really; nervous about it, just split the chickens in half and flatten slightly)
Olive oil, 6 tablespoons total, but not all together
2 tablespoons black pepper or to taste
Salt
2 tablespoons mustard, preferably the Dijon kind
1 bunch Italian parsley, leaves only
6-8 cherry tomatoes, halved
1 tablespoon sherry vinegar or cider vinegar
1 small red onion, thinly sliced (or a part thereof)
Chili oil (see below)

Chili oil:
1 cup olive oil
5 jalapeños, coarsely chopped
2 tablespoons red chili flakes

In small saucepan, combine all, bring to a simmer, and simmer 10 minutes. Remove from heat, let sit 8 hours or overnight. Strain.

Heat oven to 400°. Season chicken inside and out with salt and pepper. Brush the chicken with 2 tablespoons olive oil (not the chili oil). Place in roasting pan skin side up and roast until browned, about 30 minutes (it will be only half cooked). Meanwhile, combine 2 tablespoons olive oil, pinch salt, the mustard, and stir well. Remove chicken from oven and brush with mustard mix. Return to oven; roast until done, about 20-30 minutes longer. Let rest 10 minutes before carving. While it rests, combine parsley, red onion, and cherry tomatoes as much or as little as you like, in about equal portions. Combine remaining 2 tablespoons olive oil, 1 tablespoon vinegar and salt and pepper to taste, and toss well with salad mix. Drizzle each portion of chicken with pan juices, then chili oil and top with parsley salad.

TURKEY POLPETTONE STEAKS

2 pounds ground turkey
1 cup soft fresh bread crumbs (dried will do but fresh is better)
2 egg yolks
4 tablespoons thinly sliced green onions
1 tablespoon chopped fresh sage leaves (or 1 teaspoon dried)
1 teaspoon Worcestershire sauce
2 teaspoons salt
Freshly ground black pepper
1 tablespoon finely grated lemon zest
2 ounces Mozzarella cheese, cut into 4 equal parts, plus 2 cups
    more, grated
Olive oil for frying
1 (32-ounce) jar of your favorite marinara—I like Classico—or you
    can certainly make your own.

Preheat oven to 350°. Put turkey in a large bowl, add everything up to the mozzarella, work gently by hand, divide into 12 equal pieces, flatten each piece slightly into a round patty. Top 6 of the patties with a piece of mozzarella and then with a second patty, making 6 thick steaks. By hand, press edges together to seal and to make even thickness. Sprinkle both sides with salt and pepper. Heat a large ovenproof skillet over moderate heat; add oil to about ⅛ inch. When the oil is hot, add the patties. Cook on 1 side until lightly browned, about 1 ½ minutes, turn, cook until second side is browned, about 2 minutes. While the patties are cooking, heat the marinara in another deep skillet (or when the patties are browned, drain the oil and pour the sauce directly into that pan. It's less cleaning up to do) Put a few tablespoons of grated mozzarella on top of each patty, simmer in the marinara for about 4 minutes or until cheese is melted and patties are cooked through.

TURKEY CUTLETS DIANE

If you don't have lemon pepper, just make your own with fresh ground pepper and some grated lemon zest.

Make sauce with 2 tablespoons lemon juice, 1 tablespoon Worcestershire sauce, 1 teaspoon Dijon mustard and 1 teaspoon chopped parsley, and set aside. Sprinkle turkey cutlets with lemon pepper and sauté in butter for 3-5 minutes per side. Add sauce to pan, cook to heat, swirling the pan, and serve immediately.

SOUTHWEST TURKEY BURGER

For the salsa:
2 large tomatoes, chopped (about 2 cups)
¼ cup finely chopped red onions
2 tablespoons finely chopped fresh cilantro
1 tablespoon fresh lime juice
½ teaspoon salt

For the burger:
20 ounces lean ground turkey (in my market they sell that as a single
    package)
½ cup plain dry bread crumbs
⅓ cup finely chopped red bell pepper
2 tablespoons finely chopped green onion (scallions)
1 teaspoon chili powder
1 teaspoon ground cumin
⅓ teaspoon salt
⅛ -¼ teaspoon ground red pepper
6 large buns, toasted or not, as you like (or, if you want to dress
    them up, use 12 slices thick sliced Texas toast, from your mar-
    ket's freezer section)

Stir all the salsa ingredients together in a small bowl and set aside.

Mix well all the burger ingredients (except buns) in a medium bowl, and form into 6 patties, each about ½ inch thick.

If you want to grill these, heat the grill to medium heat. Or you can sauté them instead over medium heat in a skillet, which is what I generally do. In either case, cook them 5 to 6 minutes, turn, and cook on the other side 5-6 minutes, or until the centers are no longer pink.

Place each burger on a bun and top with salsa.

ROAST HERBED DUCK

My favorite duck recipe—it needs to be prepared ahead of time, but when you actually get around to cooking it there's not much to do.

1 tablespoon dried rosemary
1 tablespoon dried sage
1 tablespoon crushed juniper berries
1-teaspoon nutmeg
5 bay leaves
1 (5-7 pound) duck, rinsed and patted dry.
Salt and fresh ground pepper
1 cup dry vermouth
Sweet watermelon rind pickles, optional (if you can find them)

Combine rosemary, sage, juniper berries, nutmeg, and bay leaves. Grind in food processor or herb grinder, or crush in bowl, until mixed and broken into small pieces. Sprinkle the duck inside and out with salt and pepper and rub well inside and out with herb mixture. Cover and refrigerate 2-3 days). I do this in an oven roasting bag.

Heat oven to 350°. Roast on a rack 20 minutes per pound, about 2 hours. Transfer to a platter or cutting board and cover to keep warm. Pour off most of the fat and remove any burned pieces from roasting pan and place pan over medium heat. Add the wine and whisk to blend wine, fat and juices (add a little duck or chicken stock, if desired). Cut duck into serving pieces and serve with wine sauce and watermelon pickles.

If desired, toss root vegetables with olive oil, kosher salt, pepper, and minced rosemary leaves, and bake with duck (but in a separate dish) for about 1 hour or until tender, as an accompaniment.

▶*Seafood*

COOKING FISH

A great many cooks, especially beginning cooks, tend to shy away from fish. That is too bad, because most fish dishes are simplicity itself to prepare. The real difficulty is in getting good, fresh fish, and the best way to do that is to find a market that has a reliable fish department, and one that is popular, which means the fish don't sit around forever. If you can establish a good rapport with the man or woman behind the counter, so much the better. The young man at my market has been known to sniff the frozen shrimp and shake his head, meaning, "have something else for dinner."

The recipes that follow are somewhat interchangeable. You can certainly do salmon and swordfish and tuna steaks the same way. Delicate fish, like sole and, to a lesser degree, trout, are another matter.

Some years back, The Canadian Department of Fisheries worked out what I think is probably the best rule for cooking fish: measure the fish at its thickest point, and cook it for 10 minutes per inch, regardless of the cooking method. So, if a filet is half an inch thick, it will cook in 5 minutes, and a whole fish 4 inches thick will need 40. If you broil a salmon steak 1½ inches thick, you will cook it for fifteen minutes altogether, meaning you will turn it over after 7½ minutes. If you are cooking fish from frozen, double the time, or thaw it out first.

Here are some sample recipes.

BROILED SALMON STEAKS

This is a dish that is incredibly easy to prepare and delicious. If you are a beginning cook, have a go at this one. If it turns out that a guest doesn't eat fish, well, as they say in Paris, tant pis—and no, it doesn't mean that, it just means, "too bad." This can be served with just a pat of butter, or butter melted with a little dill, or you can go *grand and nap it with a Béarnaise or Hollandaise Sauce (see sauces), which makes it **Saumon en Chemise**. New potatoes with parsley and butter and some peas, minted or not, make a fine dinner, and you want a robust white wine—say a Meursault.*

2 salmon steaks, 1 inch thick
6 tablespoons melted butter
2 teaspoons lemon juice
Salt and pepper
Parsley or watercress for garnish, optional

Generously rub your grill or broiling rack with oil. Combine the butter and the lemon juice, carefully dry the steaks with paper towels, and brush them lavishly with the mixture. Place on the rack of a preheated broiler or, if grilling, use one of the hinged wire baskets. Broil or grill about 4 inches from the heat, for 5 minutes, carefully turn, brush with more of the lemon butter, sprinkle with salt and pepper, and broil 5 minutes longer.

SALMON STEAKS WITH GARLIC AND HERB BUTTER

This is much the same as above, but the garlic makes a big difference.

Make Garlic and Herb Butter: Cream 1 stick of butter (8 tablespoons) with a mixer or food processor. Beat in 1 tablespoon minced shallot or scallions, 1 teaspoon minced or pressed garlic, 2 tablespoons finely chopped parsley, salt and pepper. Set aside.

Preheat the broiler for at least 20 minutes. Dry 1 inch thick salmon steaks with paper towels, melt some butter and spread it on both sides of the salmon steaks, and broil them 3-4 inches from the heat for 2 minutes, turn and broil the other side for 2 minutes more. Baste them with more melted butter or with the drippings in the broiler pan. Salt and pepper them and broil 2 minutes more, turn, baste them again, and broil them for 4 minutes more (if they are 1 inch thick; if thicker, adjust the final broiling time accordingly). Transfer to a warm platter. Spread the garlic butter on top the steaks and garnish the platter with lemon slices.

SWORDFISH AU POIVRE (WITH PEPPER)

Again, you could do salmon or tuna steaks this same way.

2 swordfish steaks, 1½ to 2 inches thick.
1-2 tablespoons black pepper, coarsely crushed (with a rolling pin or
　a wine bottle, *e.g.*)
2 teaspoons salt
Olive oil
Chopped parsley

Press the pepper into the steaks with the heel of your hand and salt them. Brush them well with olive oil and broil 4 inches from the heat unit for 15-20 minutes total time (10 minute per inch of thickness, remember) turning once half way through the total time and brushing the tops once again with oil. Remove to a warm platter and sprinkle with the chopped parsley.

RED SNAPPER, VERACRUZ STYLE

This classic is not a dish you will prepare for yourself. It serves 6-8, and in high style, too. This recipe is based mostly on the one served at the legendary restaurant, Trader Vic's, in Oakland, and San Francisco. None of the ingredients need be exact.

Wash a 4-pound red snapper, pat dry with paper towels, and place in a large baking dish. Spread generously with softened butter and sprinkle with flour. Thinly slice 2 large tomatoes and 1 large onion, and scatter the slices atop the fish. Sprinkle with about 1 tablespoon of lime juice. Dot with some pitted ripe (black) olives, nicoise for instance, and a thinly sliced clove of garlic, sprinkle with salt and pepper, add a bay leaf to the dish and drizzle a tablespoon or two of olive oil over everything. Bake at 350° for 30-45 minutes, and garnish with parsley.

FRIED TROUT, SAN FRANCISCO STYLE

I am not about to suggest cleaning and filleting your own trout. You can get it already dressed at most fishmongers, and often frozen at your market. The simplest thing is just to bread the fish (thawed, if frozen) in a little flour seasoned with salt and pepper, or flour and cornmeal combined, and sauté it, either in butter or some bacon fat (in which case you would serve the bacon as a go-along.) Here is a somewhat dressier recipe that serves 4.

4 (10-12 ounces each) trout, cleaned, but with heads and tails left on
Salt and pepper
1 cup flour
1 cup yellow cornmeal
2 eggs
1 cup oil
8 tablespoons butter, cut into bits
¼ cup lime juice
2 tablespoons fresh chives, minced
2 tablespoons fresh parsley, finely chopped

Wash the trout and pat dry with paper towels and season inside and out with salt and pepper. Spread the flour on a sheet of waxed paper, and the cornmeal on another Beat the eggs in a shallow bowl. Heat the oil in a heavy skillet over moderate heat. Roll each trout in the flour, dip it into the egg, and then turn gently about in the cornmeal, to coat. Fry two at a time in the hot oil, 4-5 minutes for each side (remembering the 1 inch/10 minutes rule), until golden brown. Drain on paper towels and transfer to a warm platter. In a separate pan, melt the butter over moderate heat, stirring to keep it from browning. Remove from the heat, stir in the lime juice, then the chives and parsley. Pour over the trout and serve at once. If you have a chafing dish and are doing this for a dinner party, prepare the butter sauce at the table and pour it over the trout just as you are serving.

TUNA

Again, you can fix tuna steaks according to any of the recipes for salmon or swordfish.

TUNA SANDWICHES

Absolutely the most delicious tuna salad ever. Of course, you want the best tuna.

1 (7½ ounce) can Albacore Tuna, drained and flaked
1 (4½ ounce) can deviled ham
2-3 hard-boiled eggs (depending on how eggy you like it; 2 is enough for me)

¼ cup finely chopped celery
2 tablespoon dill pickle, chopped
½ teaspoon grated onion
⅓ cup mayonnaise, or more, to taste (I like a bit more in mine)
4 large hamburger buns, or 16 slices white bread if preferred
Lettuce, if desired.

Mix all ingredients and chill. Spread on buns, top with lettuce. Makes 4 large sandwiches, or 8 if you use sliced bread. Optional— top with potato chips.

THE TUNA CASSEROLE

Unless you grew up on the moon, you must have encountered this casserole somewhere along the way. Surprisingly, though, I looked through a number of cookbooks without finding a recipe—I suppose today's more sophisticated cooks look down their noses at it, but I still think it's awfully good. Now, there is an idea today that tuna in water is better for you. Pish, posh. It has no taste. Buy tuna in oil (if you can find belly meat, sometimes labeled ventresca, and usually from Spain or Italy, that is the very best, but I think that is better saved to toss simply with some pasta and maybe a tomato or two and some capers) and drain it thoroughly, the nutritional difference will be infinitesimal. If you are really anal, you can rinse it under running water, too, but, really…

1 can (10½ ounces) cream of mushroom soup—oh, be fair, it's
    Campbell's recipe, use their soup, for Pete's sake)
⅓ cup milk
1 (7-ounce) can tuna, drained and flaked
2 cups (about) cooked noodles
2 hard cooked eggs, sliced
1 cup cooked peas (or frozen, don't even bother to thaw them)
1 cup potato chips, slightly crumbled, but don't make dust of them.

Combine well the soup and milk in a 1 quart baking dish. Stir in the tuna, noodles, eggs and the peas, and top with the chips. Bake at 350° for 30 minutes. You can vary this by using cream of celery or cream of chicken soup, and instead of peas, you could certainly use green beans, asparagus or artichoke hearts. This isn't rocket science.

SOLE MUNIÈRE

First, I must explain about sole—there isn't any. Well, there is, and it's properly called Dover sole, because that is where it is from, and if you could find it at your market, the price would surely give you cardiac arrest. What you will find, labeled sole, is flounder, and it is sold either as lemon sole (better) or gray sole (okay). You can use either for this dish, which is the classic French way to cook sole, as it brings out the delicate flavor.

Coat sole filets with flour and brown in hot butter over medium heat, turning once. Salt and pepper and remove filets to a warm platter. Turn up the heat and brown the butter in the pan, being careful not to let it burn. Pour over the fish, sprinkle with a little lemon juice and chopped parsley, and serve at once.

FILET OF SOLE EN CASSEROLE

The combination of sole, mushrooms (which contain a natural form of MSG), and white wine is classic. There are countless variations on this dish, some of them quite complicated. This one is relatively simple, and simply delicious.

Butter—you will need, at different times, 7 tablespoons in all
2 tablespoons finely chopped shallots
4 boneless, skinless sole filets, about 1 to 1½ pounds
6-8 button mushrooms, trimmed of stems
1 teaspoon salt
⅛ teaspoon pepper (white is better, but don't get hysterical)
¼ cup dry vermouth
2 tablespoons bottled clam juice
⅓ cup water
2 tablespoons flour
1 cup heavy cream
1 egg yolk
1 teaspoon chopped parsley, or other herb of your choice.

Preheat the oven to 350°. Grease a large, ovenproof skillet with 2 teaspoons of butter. Cut a sheet of parchment paper to fit on top of the skillet, and grease that with 1 teaspoon butter. Sprinkle 1 table-spoon of the shallots into the bottom of the skillet.

Fold the ends of the filets under, place them smooth side up in the skillet and sprinkle with salt and pepper and the remaining tablespoon of shallots. Scatter the mushrooms about the fish. Cut 2 tablespoons of butter in small pieces and dot the filets with them. Pour the vermouth, the clam juice and the water around the fish. Over medium high heat, bring to a simmer, and place the parchment paper, buttered side down, over the fish.

Place the skillet in the oven and bake until barely cooked through, 6-10 minutes, depending upon the thickness of the folded filets (10 minutes per inch, but it is far better to undercook than to overcook; they will finish cooking while you make the sauce). While the fish is baking, heat three tablespoons butter in a small saucepan over medium-low heat, and blend in the flour. Cook, stirring, for 2 minutes, and set aside.

When the fish is done, remove it with the mushrooms to a warmed platter and cover with foil to keep warm. Add the fish cooking liquid and ½ cup of the cream to the butter/flour roux, return to the heat and cook, stirring, until thickened. Mix the remaining ½ cup cream with the egg yolk, pour a small amount of the sauce over this to heat the egg, and then add this all back into the sauce and cook, stirring constantly, for 3-4 minutes more, until thick and glossy. Add remaining 1 tablespoon of butter to the sauce, adjust seasoning, cloak the fish lightly with it, sprinkle the chopped parsley on top and serve the remaining sauce on the side.

You can substitute another herb—say, tarragon—for the parsley if you like. You can also put the fish in an ovenproof casserole when you take it from the skillet, and when the sauce is done, coat the fish with some of it and brown briefly under a broiler, then sprinkle it with your herb, and serve the rest of the sauce on the side—but I personally don't find that it needs this extra step, and you do risk overcooking the fish.

Now, suppose you have, despite my advice, overcooked the fish and it is falling apart. Don't despair. Keep it warm and quickly cook some linguini. Put the drained linguini on a platter (or individual plates) and pour the fish and its sauce over, and serve it for all the world as if that's what you had in mind all along. Who will know? Oh, well, tell him to keep his mouth shut for a change.

SHELLFISH: SHRIMP

The best way to cook shrimp is to shell and devein them first and then steam them over very low heat. Choose a large deep skillet or pot with a lid and a steaming apparatus. Arrange the shrimp in a single layer so they cook evenly; it's easy to do several batches. Heat a small amount of water in the pot (with low heat, you don't need much water). Once the water starts to simmer, turn the heat as low as possible, set the shrimp filled steamer basket in the pot, cover and cook until the shrimp just turn opaque. Medium shrimp (31-35 count) generally are fully cooked in 4-5 minutes. Large shrimp (21-25 count) steam in 5½-6 minutes. Jumbo (16-20) take 6-7 minutes Set the timer for the lesser time and check; Shrimp should be firm, completely opaque and bright coral. If not, set the timer for another minute and check again. If in doubt, cover the pot, turn off the heat and let the residual heat gently finish cooking the shrimp. If you add some pickling spices to the water to begin, they will lend the shrimp a nice flavor, but it is not necessary.

CLASSIC COCKTAIL SAUCE FOR SHRIMP

Combine:
1 cup chili sauce
1 teaspoon to 1 tablespoon prepared horseradish, or to taste (I like more)
1 tablespoon lemon juice, or more to taste
½ teaspoon grated lemon zest
¼ teaspoon grated onion
3 tablespoons burgundy or other dry red wine
Black pepper

LEMON PARSLEY CAPER MAYONNAISE FOR SHRIMP

½ cup mayonnaise
1 cup minced parsley leaves
1 tablespoons lemon juice
½ teaspoon grated lemon zest
2 scallions, minced
¼ cup drained capers, finely chopped

SHRIMP IN RUM

Peel and devein 24 large shrimp, leaving tails on. Split lengthwise without cutting them all the way through, so they remain attached at the tail. Arrange them standing up (tails up—isn't this fun?) in a baking pan. Pour rum-butter sauce (below) over shrimp. Bake in preheated 450°-oven for 4 minutes, slip under broiler for 2-3 minutes more to brown. Remove to bed of hot rice in serving dish. Drain off sauce; combine with an additional jigger dark rum, spoon over shrimp and rice. Don't eat this and drive.

Rum Butter Sauce: mince 2 cloves garlic and combine with 1 tablespoon chopped parsley, 1 teaspoon oregano, ½ teaspoon salt, 2 tablespoons lemon juice, ½ cup melted butter, 1 jigger dark rum.

WHOLE LOBSTER

If you're squeamish about putting a struggling lobster in a pot of boiling water, you can first put him in your freezer for 5-10 minutes to sedate him. Or, just pretend that he is your ex.

To Boil: bring about one gallon heavily salted water to boil. Add live lobster, cook 10 minutes for first pound and 2 minutes more for each additional ¼ pound, up to 3 pounds.

To steam: bring 1-2 inches water to rolling boil. Place lobster on rack above water, cook 10 minutes for the first pound, 2 minutes more for each additional ¼ pound, up to 3 pounds.

WHOLE CRAB

To select crabs, choose ones that feel heavy for their size. Make sure the merchant lets the crabs drain before weighing, as they can retain a fair amount of water. Best crabs are dark in color. Light color legs mean it has recently molted and won't be as meaty. Pinch a leg if you can, to make sure it feels full of meat and not flimsy. Unless you know your fishmonger, do not let him turn away to wrap the crabs—I have gotten home to find that all the claws had vanished.

To steam; heat about 2 cups water in large pot, bring to boil; place live 1½-2-pound crab on steaming rack above water, cover tightly, steam for 10 minutes; remove, crack and clean, removing the Dead Man's Fingers, or spongy gills on either side of the body. Serve with melted butter or your preferred sauce. To steam more than 1 crab, add 3 minutes for each additional 1½ pounds, up to 15 minutes. Make sure crabs are about the same weight.

Or: put 1 cup wine, 2 cups water, a bay leaf, black peppercorns and 1 lemon cut in wedges. Optional: 1 sliced onion, knob of ginger sliced, 1 tablespoon pickling spice. Bring to boil, add live crabs, cover, reduce heat, and simmer 10-12 minutes.

OVEN-BRAISED CRAB

There's no question about it, this is messy. I suggest covering the cocktail table in newspapers, give yourself a roll of paper towels, and sit on the floor while you savor this. It needs nothing more than some good sourdough bread and a green salad.

1 crab (uncooked is best; if you can only get cooked, adjust the timing, below); ask the fishmonger to kill and dress the crab
½ stick butter
¼ cup olive oil
2 tablespoons minced garlic
1 tablespoon minced shallot
1½ teaspoons dried crushed red pepper
2 tablespoon chopped parsley, separated
½ cup orange juice
1 teaspoon grated orange peel
1 teaspoon fresh thyme leaves

Heat oven to 500°. Melt butter and oil in large ovenproof skillet over medium high heat. Stir in garlic, shallots and pepper. Add crabs, sprinkle with salt and pepper and 1 tablespoon chopped parsley, place in oven about 15 minutes, stirring once. (If the crab was pre-cooked, reduce cooking time to 5 minutes.) Put crab on platter, keep warm. Add orange juice and grated peel to the pan and boil on top the stove to reduce liquid by half, about 5 minutes. Pour over crab, sprinkle with thyme and remaining parsley.

CRAB DIPPING SAUCE

½ cup yellow crab butter (optional)—from cooked crab, press through sieve
½ cup mayonnaise
½ teaspoon steak sauce
½ teaspoon of your favorite liqueur or liquor (Scotch works well)

CRAB CAKES

1 pound lump crabmeat, drained and picked over carefully
1 egg, slightly beaten
½ teaspoon dry mustard
1-2 dashes Worcestershire sauce
4 unsalted soda crackers (saltines) crushed.
1 onion (preferably Vidalia or other sweet onion) chopped
½ green pepper, chopped
1-2 teaspoons chopped parsley
Salt and pepper to taste
2 eggs, beaten with 1 tablespoon of cold water
Butter and oil for frying
Breadcrumbs, seasoned or plain, as you prefer

Combine everything up to the eggs. Form cakes and place on waxed paper on cookie sheet (this should make about 12 cakes.) Immediately refrigerate and chill to harden, 2 hours or more.

When ready to serve, beat the eggs in shallow bowl and spread the crumbs in another, or on waxed paper. Melt 1-2 tablespoon butter and 1-2 tablespoon oil in large skillet over medium heat. Work with half the crab cakes at a time, leaving second half in the refrigerator until ready to cook. Dip each cake into eggs and coat with breadcrumbs *(note: you can prepare cakes to this point and freeze)*. Sauté until browned, 2-3 minutes each side—turn only once to avoid breaking. Drain on paper towels and serve, with tarter sauce, mayonnaise or aioli.

VICTOR'S CIOPPINO

This is sloppy and gloppy and oh, so good. It takes some advance preparation but really isn't that difficult once you get started—it's more a matter of timing. Despite the Italian name, Cioppino is actually "a San Francisco treat," but of course, recipes are like story plots, they've all been used before, it just a matter of variation. There are endless kinds of fish stews all around the Mediterranean; this is just a California version.

1 cooked Dungeness crab (or substitute lobster or King crab legs)*
1 pound or more jumbo shrimp (I use frozen peeled deveined shrimp, thawed in cold water) (you can add clams, mussels, or even oysters, if desired)

1½ cups chopped onion
½ cup to 1 cup chopped green pepper
3 cloves garlic, peeled and put through a press
½ cup olive oil
1 large can (28 ounces) tomatoes (you can use the crushed, but I like the whole ones, and mash them a bit with a fork or a potato masher)
2 cups red table wine (Beaujolais or Zinfandel, *e.g.*)
2 cups tomato juice
2 cups of the stock from cooking the crab, or use bottled clam juice
1 bay leaf
1 teaspoon dried basil
1 tablespoon chopped parsley (see below)
Salt and pepper to taste
1 or 2 pounds of sea bass, halibut or other firm fish
Additional chopped parsley for garnish.

Sauté the onion, green pepper, and garlic in the olive oil, just until soft, don't brown. Add the tomatoes. If you are using clams, etc, add their juices now. Then add the red wine, the tomato juice, and the crab stock or clam juice, the bay leaf, basil, parsley and salt and pepper. Cook gently about 30 minutes, taste for seasoning. You can prepare this ahead and reheat it when you're about ready to serve.

About 8-10 minutes before you plan to serve this, add the fish. About 2 minutes after that, add the crab. In about 2 more minutes, add the shrimp, and cook for five minutes.

Sprinkle with about 2 tablespoon more chopped parsley, and freshly grated Parmesan if desired. Serve with garlic toast and a salad and, ideally, nutcrackers and picks. And lots of towels.

*To cook a whole crab to eat as is—*i.e.*, rather than to use in a Cioppino—steam it according to the directions above or cook 20 minutes in boiling salted water; however, for this cioppino, cook it for only 15 minutes, rinse under cold running water to stop the cooking. Save some of the cooking broth (see above.) Break off legs and claws. Break the small triangular "apron" off the crab's underside. Pull of the back (upper shell.) Remove the gills (the spongy, sort of finger like stuff on each side of the body). This will leave you a body sort of like a honeycomb. The meat inside each section has to be picked out, but is delicious. If you're making Cioppino, however, don't pick it out now. Rinse the body under running water to clean off fat, green liver, etc. Break body in 2 pieces. Refrigerate crab sections or keep cool until ready to add to pot.

J. D.'s CIOPPINO

Since I already had my own Cioppino recipe in the book, I initially thought when Joseph de Marco sent this one that I would pass on it—but when I read it, it sounded so delicious, and more authentically Italian (well, de Marco, duh), I thought I had to include this one as well. I feel sure if you try either one, you will be so intrigued, you'll want to try the other as well. Joe writes:

"When I made this dish the first time, I'd never made cioppino before. I know what they say about first time dishes and guests. But I decided to fly in the face of that advice and try something new on a bunch of old friends. After all, I thought at the time, it's an Italian dish, I'm Italian, how hard could it be?

"I'm happy to say that I was right. The dish is time-consuming, however. The preparation takes a bit of time and effort but the cooking is relatively quick. So be prepared for some quality time with your cutting board, squid innards, and other messy things.

"Before we get started, a little advice: this is not a cheap dish. So you'd better really like the people you're feeding.

"There are lots of versions of this Italian fish stew. The one here is my own take on what to include and how to prepare it. I like a red sauce version (being Southern Italian). And it makes for a very pretty mix.

"If you're going to do seafood stew, then it should be rich in ingredients. And good, fresh ingredients at that. I like to include a little of everything: some items will 'disappear' into the mix leaving behind their unmistakable essence and contributing to a stew that is heavenly and won't be forgotten. Some ingredients will attempt to steal the show—that's all right. Let them be their showy selves, it will make your dish all the more visually appealing. Other ingredients will be the staples, the pillars on which everything else rests. That's cioppino to me—more than a stew. It's a work of culinary art."

The stars of the dish—the seafood:
1½ pounds (cleaned) squid (and make sure you get plenty of tentacles, that's the fun part)
1½ pounds shrimp (not the tiny ones but not the gargantuan ones either)
1 pound scallops (sea or bay—your choice if you get the bigger ones make it 2 pounds)

Lobster tail—two small ones will do—for the taste and for the look
(you're going to leave the whole thing in but at the very end get
the meat out into the stew and leave the shell for garnish)
½ pound crabmeat
2 pounds mussels (in the shell—green or black or both)
1 pound clams (some shelled and again to make the dish visually
impressive leave some in their shells)
½ pound tilapia or rock fish or some other firm white fish
½ pound cod
½ pound halibut or haddock (optional)
AND any other sea creature you'd like to add to the mix, like sea
cucumbers or octopus perhaps.

Next, the supporting players:
2-3 tablespoons Extra Virgin Olive Oil *(see my introductory notes—
VJB)*
6 cloves garlic or more depending on your taste (finely sliced or
minced)
8-16 ounces clam juice (or a bit more—use your judgment)
1-2 cups fish stock (you can buy a bottled brand, Better Than Fish
Bouillon, in most supermarkets or accumulate some scraps and
make your own)
2-3 teaspoons basil (maybe more if you like)
1 teaspoon oregano
1½ cups chopped flat leaf parsley
Salt to taste
1 large onion diced
Several stalks of celery and the leafy matter, too (it will add flavor)
2 or 3 carrots (optional)
1 each green, red, and yellow bell peppers diced
2-3 bay leaves
1 cup dry white wine
1 container mushrooms—plain old mushrooms—but this is optional
1-2 large cans (32 ounces) crushed tomatoes (or you can get a couple of pounds of plum tomatoes and crush them yourself)
1-2 large cans (16 ounces) tomato sauce—you may find that you'll
need more tomato sauce

Now for the preparation:
First assemble all your fishy ingredients, wash and clean them
and get them ready to go.
The squid will be the biggest challenge, because even if your
fishmonger takes out the inner workings including the nice little ink

sac, there are still some things you'll need to pull out. Like that piece of cartilage that looks like a plastic tag or some such thing. You don't want guests thinking you dropped plastic bits into the stew. Then you'll want to slice the squid into neat circles. Leave the tentacles intact. They look great in the dish and they are a meaty delight.

The mussels need to be de-bearded and washed (sandy ingredients are a no-no). If you'd rather leave the mussels out, it won't hurt the dish and will save you a little time. If you do use mussels, remember: If the shell does not partly open when cooked, Throw It Out! (Unless this is a "get even" dinner party.)

The rest of the fish are easy to deal with (okay, the shrimp may take a little time if you forgot to get them shelled). Just make certain everything is clean and ready to go.

The cod, halibut, rockfish, *etc.* should be chopped into medium-sized pieces.

The lobster tails go in as is—loosen and release the meat at the end of the cooking.

Clean the clams well to get rid of grit. If you find a pearl, remember who gave you this recipe.

Pour the oil into a large stew pot and sauté the garlic-not too long. Throw in the onion and let that heady mix entertain your nostrils for a while. Once the onions are translucent, you can add the tomato sauce and the crushed tomatoes. Stir it up and add the spices, the carrots (if you're using them), half of the parsley, the basil and the bay leaf. Let it simmer for a bit. Then add the bell peppers, the white wine, and the mushrooms (if you are including them).

Let this simmer for about 10 minutes. Then turn up the heat slightly for the rest of the ingredients.

Add the lobster tails, the cod, the other white fish, the crabmeat. After five or more minutes, add the clams and mussels and let them cook. Next—and these should all be last so as not to make a rubbery mess—add the scallops, the squid, and the shrimp. You won't want these to cook too long. Five minutes (maybe a little more if you want to be certain, but not much). Watch them change color and consistency.

Then turn off the heat and let it "rest" on the stove for a few minutes before you serve it.

When you serve, throw the rest of the parsley on top, make certain the lobster tails are showing along with a squid tentacle or two and the clam and mussel shells are arranged nicely around the edges. You've spent a lot of time and money on this dish. It needs to look good on the table.

At the same time as you started this stew, make some rice. Brown rice is good and so is white rice. I like having something to put the stew over and rice is perfect.

You'll want to have some crusty bread on the table and a veggie or two to round it all out (asparagus goes well with this).

The wine is your choice. I don't tend to follow wine rules.

This should serve at least 8 people with lots of leftovers to freeze for a rainy day.

▶ *Pork*

VICTOR'S UNBELIEVABLY DELICIOUS ROAST PORK

For years my friend Todd Clark was the only one with whom I shared this recipe, and he often urged me to open a sandwich shop selling nothing but sandwiches made from this pork. The years pass, however, and friends began to urge me to share this recipe, lest something happen and it be lost. So, here it is. It can be served hot, but frankly, I like it better at room temperature, and it is particularly good with the Chili Mayo (see the section on sauces). This is best cooked on a rotisserie, which allows the meat to baste itself constantly and results in a moister roast, but I have done it quite successfully in a conventional oven, though I generally either turn it over a time or two while roasting, or baste it often with the pan juices, to keep it moist.

3-4-pound pork tenderloin (or boneless loin roast, tied)
6-7 cups water
1 cup sugar
6 tablespoons chili powder
2 tablespoons salt
2 tablespoons crushed dried thyme
1 tablespoon ground cumin
2 teaspoons coarsely ground black pepper
2 teaspoons crushed oregano

Heat everything except the pork to boiling in a large saucepan, stirring to dissolve and mix thoroughly. Remove from heat and cool to room temperature. Place meat in a non-reactive container (not metal) large enough to immerse the pork in cure solution, (Or place in 2 gallon self sealing plastic bag and place that in any kind of container large enough to hold it.) If brine does not quite cover the meat, add another cup of water. Cover and refrigerate at least 24 hours. 3 days is ideal.

Remove loin from marinade and discard marinade. Pat pork gently dry with paper towels, cook on rotisserie or roast in a 350° oven for 1½-1¾ hours, to internal temperature of 160°. If cooked in the oven, baste or turn as directed above, and I like to turn the oven up to 475° for the last twenty minutes or so to brown the edges. Serve hot or at room temperature (I think that is best). Serve with Chili Mayo

PORK CHOPS CHARCUTIÈRE

This is an old fashioned recipe, and a bit fussy by today's standards, but I think it holds up pretty well. Charcutière means in the butcher's style.

6 loin pork chops, 1 inch thick
3 tablespoons oil
¼ cup minced onion
¼ cup dry white wine
½ tablespoon tarragon vinegar
1 cup beef broth
¼ cup tomato purée
1 tablespoon flour
1 teaspoon dry mustard
Salt and pepper
2 tablespoons minced dill pickle
2 tablespoon chopped fresh parsley

Brown the chops on both sides in 2 tablespoons of the oil. Reduce heat, cover and cook for about 45 minutes or until done, turning once. Meanwhile, make the sauce: in a separate pan, sauté the onion in the remaining tablespoon oil, until golden. Add wine and vinegar and cook, stirring occasionally, for five minutes or until nearly all the liquid has evaporated. Stir in ½ cup broth and the tomato purée. Combine remaining broth with flour and mustard and whisk until smooth. Stir into the hot sauce, bring to a boil, reduce heat, and simmer uncovered for 30 minutes, stirring from time to time. Taste for seasoning and add salt and pepper if needed. When chops are done, remove to a platter, cover to keep warm. Stir pickle and parsley into sauce and cook 2-3 minutes over low heat—do not boil. Pour over chops.

CREOLE-STYLE PORK STEW

This is luscious, with a complex blend of flavors. There's a bit of chopping, etc., to start, but once you put it on to simmer it doesn't really need any attention and it can even be made a day or two ahead. You can serve this over rice, gumbo style, or over noodles, or just in bowls as a stew. Vary the herbs as you like; I have used marjoram and rosemary in place of the sage and oregano. Likewise alter the cayenne to taste.

½ cup oil
½ cup flour
2 cups chopped onion (1 large)
1 cup chopped celery
1 medium green bell pepper, chopped (if peppers bother you, substitute a chopped carrot)
1 pound (about) of Andouille, Lingüiça, or other sausage
2 tablespoons minced garlic, about 4 large cloves
4 cups chicken stock (1 32-ounce carton)
2 tablespoons tomato paste
1 tablespoon Worcestershire
2 bay leaves
½ teaspoon dried sage
½ teaspoon oregano
½-1 teaspoon cayenne
2 pounds boneless country style pork ribs, cut into roughly 1½ inch pieces
Kosher salt, fresh pepper
Hot pepper sauce, optional
Rice (optional, see above)

Chop about half the sausage coarsely; cut the rest into slices or meaty chunks. Make a roux: heat oil in large, heavy pot over medium low heat, cook the flour in it, stirring often, until it turns a rich red-brown color, about 20-25 minutes. Watch carefully and stir constantly towards the end as, like caramel, once it starts to darken it can go really dark really fast. Remove from heat and carefully stir in the onion, celery, bell pepper and the chopped sausage. Return pot to medium heat, cook and stir 5 minutes. Yes, it will look funny. Stir in garlic, then the chicken stock and tomato paste. Then add the Worcestershire, bay leaves, herbs and cayenne. Bring to a boil over high heat. Add the pork, reduce heat and simmer uncovered for about 1½-2 hours, till the pork is tender and the stock is thickened as you want it (thicker if you are skipping the rice, *e.g.*, and serving it just as a stew). Stir in remaining sausage, cook 5 minutes longer to heat through (at this point the stew can be cooled and refrigerated up to 2 days, and reheated when you are ready to serve). Discard bay leaves, skim off any excess fat, and add salt, pepper and hot pepper sauce to taste. Spoon over rice if desired.

TOMATO ONION PORK CHOPS

An easy dish for the neophyte. Serve this with rice or noodles and a green vegetable—buy a frozen pre-sauced one, like Brussels sprouts. No one will guess you can't cook.

1 tablespoon oil
4 center cut pork chops, ½ inch thick
1 medium onion, chopped
1 cup water
1 package Knorr dry tomato basil soup mix
¼ cup brown sugar
4 teaspoons Worcestershire sauce

In large skillet, heat oil over medium high heat. Add chops and onion and brown, turning occasionally, about 5 minutes. Set chops aside. Add remaining ingredients. Stirring constantly, bring to a boil. Return chops to skillet. Reduce heat, cover, simmer 20-30 minutes or until tender.

BUFFET HAM

Forget about elaborate, grand hams for your buffet table Buy a cheap one at the market, and prepare it as below, and your guests will think it's the best they ever had. If you want to dress it up, get some candied fruit, say red and green maraschino cherries, and make star patterns on the top of the ham. Before you start, make sure you have a pan large enough to hold a ham this big (of course, you can do a smaller ham, too)

Heat oven to 300°. Trim tough outer skin and excess fat from a 15-pound smoked ham on the bone. Place ham, meat side down, in large roasting pan and score top, making crosshatch incisions with sharp knife. Roast 2 hours. Remove ham from oven and increase heat to 350°. Meanwhile, for the glaze, combine ¾ cup orange marmalade (diabetics can do this with sugar free marmalade, it's still delicious), ½ cup Dijon mustard and ¾ cup firmly packed brown sugar in medium bowl. Stud ham with about 1 tablespoon of whole cloves, brush generously with glaze and return to oven. Cook another 1½ hours, brushing with glaze at least 3 times. Transfer to cutting board or platter and allow to rest about 30 minutes.

EASY OVEN SPARERIBS

Too often marinades overpower the delicious flavor of the ribs themselves. Better to brush, as here, with mustard (Dijon is great, but even the ballpark stuff will do) and then use a dry rub like this one or, if you feel hurried or lazy, there are some nice ones in the market. Forget about parboiling the ribs first and don't even think about trying to hurry them along at a higher temperature. Don't use a pan, either, roast them right on the oven rack. You can spray it first with non-stick spray if you like, and it will wash up with soap and water. If you must have a barbecue sauce, serve it on the side for dipping. I like them just as they are. If you have a gas oven, you can roast on both racks, but with an electric oven, the heating element is on the oven floor, and you must place your foil lined pan on the lower rack, so you can only do the ribs on one, but you can still do this full recipe (with gas, you can double it).

6 tablespoons brown sugar
6 tablespoons paprika
3 tablespoons fresh ground pepper
3 tablespoons garlic powder
1½ teaspoons salt
9 tablespoons Dijon or yellow mustard (½ cup plus 1 tablespoon)
2 teaspoons liquid smoke
2 slabs (9 pounds) of pork spareribs, or 4 slabs (8 pounds) of baby back ribs

Adjust top oven rack to upper middle position and preheat oven to 250°. Mix the sugar, paprika, pepper, garlic powder and salt. In another bowl, combine mustard and optional liquid smoke. Brush both sides of the ribs with mustard, and then sprinkle both sides with the dry rub (it really doesn't have to be rubbed.)

Line a large jellyroll pan or other shallow roasting pan with heavy-duty foil—this is to catch the drippings. If you have a gas oven, place the pan on the oven floor. If electric, place the pan on the bottom oven rack. In either case, be sure the foil covers the entire oven level. Roast until the ribs are fork tender—2-3 hours for spare ribs and 1½-2 hours for baby backs.

This produces ribs with a slight crunchy. Some people prefer the soft kind of fall-off-the-bone tender meat that comes from steaming. If that is your preferences, for the last hour of cooking, wrap the ribs in foil and place them in a brown paper bag.

PLAIN AND SIMPLE OVEN-ROASTED PORK SPARERIBS

When all is said and done, I think this is my favorite recipe for spareribs. You can do beef spareribs the same way.

2 sides of pork spareribs, about 4 pounds altogether
Coarse kosher salt
Freshly ground black pepper

Preheat the oven to 350°. Place the ribs on a rack in a shallow roasting pan, and roast 30 minutes. Take them from the oven and season them generously with the salt and pepper; turn them over and season the other side as well, put them back in the oven and roast for another 30 minutes. Turn them again and roast for another thirty minutes, until browned and fairly crisp. If you like them well browned and crispy, you can crank the heat up for the last 30 minutes, say to 425°. Remove from the oven, place on a cutting board and cut the ribs into small serving pieces. Serves 4.

▶ *Beef*

ROAST BEEF THE EASY WAY

You can do any kind of beef roast by this method. If you're looking for a centerpiece for a holiday buffet, and unless you want to garnish yourself with parsley and lay on the table, you can't get much easier than doing an eye of round or a tenderloin this way. It's best sliced very thin, and I like to leave one end unsliced, so the piggish guests will get discouraged and leave me some for next day. If you don't have a meat-slicer and are not good at thin-slicing, try making eyes at your butcher and maybe he'll slice it for you. Mine threatened to trim my rump with a cleaver, but that's another story.

Heat oven to 500°. Roast beef for 5 minutes per pound. Turn off oven, let roast sit undisturbed for 1-1½ hours. If you like, you can rub the meat before roasting with the seasoning salt (in the Sauces section) or combine 1 cup salt, ¼ cup pepper, and ¼ cup garlic powder, and season with that before roasting.

FOOLPROOF STANDING RIB ROAST

This works regardless of size, so the timing is simpler, but the result is the same.

One 5-pound rib roast (but the weight really doesn't matter)

Allow roast to stand at room temperature for at least 1 hour, and season as above, if desired. Preheat oven to 375°. Place on rack in pan, rib side down. Roast 1 hour Turn off oven. Leave roast in oven but do not open door. Let sit for at least 1 hour. About 30-40 minutes before serving time, turn oven to 375° and reheat. Do not remove roast or open door from time roast is first put into oven until ready to serve

ROAST PRIME RIB, ENGLISH STYLE

A more traditional approach. This benefits from basting, which you cannot do with either of the above recipes.

Let roast come to room temperature. Heat oven to 450°. Combine 3 tablespoons flour, 1 tablespoon dry mustard, 1 teaspoon salt, and 2 teaspoons black pepper, mix well, rub all over roast. Place fat side up in large roasting pan. Put oven rack at the lowest level and roast the beef for 20 minutes. Reduce heat to 325° and roast 15 minutes per pound, basting frequently with pan juices. After 1 hour and 45 minutes, pour 1 cup dry red wine over meat. Continue roasting and basting until the temperature on an instant read meat thermometer reads 120° for medium rare. Remove from oven, allow to rest 30 minutes.

SEARED ROASTED RIB STEAK WITH GARLIC BUTTER

You should have an exhaust fan to do this, as it will make the kitchen smoky. Otherwise, do it with a couple of windows open. It's worth the nuisance, however.

3 garlic cloves
Kosher salt
8 tablespoons unsalted butter, softened
1 teaspoon dried thyme
Generous pinch black pepper
2 tablespoons vegetable oil
2 large (16-20 ounces) or 4 small (8-10 ounces) bone-in rib steaks or
    boneless rib eyes, at least 1 inch thick

Chop garlic fine. Sprinkle 1 tablespoon salt over garlic and continue to chop, smashing and smearing to a paste (or you can combine them and smash and smoosh them around with the flat bottom of a glass or a ramekin.) Put garlic paste, butter, thyme, and pepper in small bowl. Fold butter over and onto garlic, mashing with the back of a spoon. Use a sheet of Saran wrap to help shape into a log, wrap well with Saran and refrigerate until ready to use. Can be made 3 days ahead, or frozen for a couple of months.

Melt half the garlic butter mixture in a small pan over medium heat and set aside. Heat oven to 425°. In large ovenproof pan or skillet, heat vegetable oil on the stovetop over high heat until very hot.

Season steaks with salt and pepper. Add to the pan, brown well on 1 side, about 5 minutes. Turn steaks and brush liberally with garlic butter. Transfer the pan to the oven and finish cooking in the oven, brushing occasionally with more garlic butter, until done, about another 5 minutes. Remove from oven, allow to rest 5 minutes. Serve whole or slice across the grain. Spoon any remaining juices from the pan onto the meat.

TEX MEX BURGERS

1 pound ground chuck
1 jalapeño, seeded and minced (it's best to wear gloves; in any case, be sure to wash your hands thoroughly afterward to avoid getting it in your eyes, *etc.*)
1 cup spicy tomato salsa (buy it pre-made)
Salt and fresh pepper
1 ripe avocado, pitted and sliced
½ cup shredded sharp Cheddar
4 soft corn tortillas (if you're fond of buns, you can use them instead)

Preheat broiler or grill to medium high. Using a wooden spoon (or wear gloves and do by hand) mix beef, jalapeño, ¼ cup salsa, salt and pepper. Form into 4 patties, a little flatter and greater in diameter than usual burger shape. Broil or grill, flipping once, until cooked through, about 4 minutes per side. If using tortillas, place two at a time in microwave and cook on high about 20 seconds. Arrange each burger on a warm tortilla (or bun), top with avocado, cheese and additional salsa, or wrap like burritos. Serve with additional salsa and red beans and rice.

SWISS STEAK

There are a zillion recipes for Swiss steak. I like this one, and it's easy.

1 round steak approximately 1½ pounds; it can be cubed or pounded for tenderness, but I think that is just extra bother
1 teaspoon garlic powder
Salt and pepper
Flour for dusting
⅓ cup oil

2 cloves garlic, crushed
1 (14½ ounce) can diced tomatoes
1 medium onion in strips, sautéed or not.
1 medium bell pepper, in strips (Optional)

Cut steak into serving size pieces. Season with garlic salt and pepper, dust with flour (A lot of older recipes recommend pounding the flour into the meat with the edge of a saucer, but I never did see what that accomplished either.) Brown both sides in oil. Combine remaining ingredients and 1 tomato can of water, pour over steak, and simmer until meat is tender, 1-1½ hours. Check for seasoning. Water can be used instead of tomatoes, or bouillon, or red wine. Mushrooms can be sautéed and added when meat is almost done. Green peas also. Celery can be sautéed and added with the onions. Carrots, turnips, herbs, this is nothing if not forgiving. Serve with noodles or mashed potatoes

VICTOR'S CHILI

This is my favorite chili recipe—a bit of work, but worth it.

3 pounds top round of beef cut into ½ inch cubes
6 tablespoons oil
2 cups coarsely chopped onion
2 tablespoons finely chopped garlic
4 tablespoons chili powder or to taste
1 teaspoon oregano
1 teaspoon cumin
1 teaspoon red pepper flakes
1 six-ounce can tomato paste
4 cups beef stock
1 teaspoon salt
Fresh black pepper
1½ cups drained kidney beans, optional

Pat meat dry with paper towels. In a 12" heavy skillet, heat 4 tablespoons of oil until a light haze forms above it. Add meat and cook on high 2-3 minutes, stirring, until meat is lightly browned. With slotted spoon, transfer meat to a 4-quart heavy casserole. Add remaining 1 tablespoon oil to skillet, cook onion and garlic 4-5 minutes, stirring frequently. Remove skillet from heat; add chili powder, oregano, cumin, pepper flakes, and stir until onions are well coated. Then add tomato paste, pour in the beef stock and mix ingredients thoroughly before adding to the meat in the casserole. Add salt and pepper. Bring to a boil; stirring once or twice, then half-cover pot, turn heat to low and simmer 1-1½ hours or until meat is tender. Add beans 15 minutes or so before meat is done. Skim as much surface fat as you can.

SUPER CHOPPED STEAK

½ pound lean ground beef
2 scallions (3 inches of green left on), thinly sliced
1 tablespoon chopped flat leaf parsley
2 teaspoons fresh lemon juice
2 teaspoons soy sauce, plus extra for cooking
Salt and fresh black pepper
1 tablespoon olive oil
Sliced tomato (optional)

Gently combine beef, scallions, parsley lemon juice, 2 teaspoons soy sauce, salt and pepper. Form into patties, about 3 inches in diameter and 1½ inch thick. Heat olive oil in non-stick skillet over medium heat. Cook patties 5 minutes, turn and cook 3 minutes for medium rare, brushing patties on second side with soy sauce. Serve immediately with sliced tomatoes if desired.

FILET OF BEEF WITH BLUE CHEESE SAUCE

Preheat oven to 500°. Melt 2 tablespoons unsalted butter. Place 1½ pound fillet, trimmed and tied, on baking sheet, pat dry with paper towels. Use pastry brush to coat beef with butter. Sprinkle with salt and pepper. Roast 25 minutes for medium rare. Remove from oven, cover tightly with foil and let rest at room temp 20 minutes. Serve with blue cheese sauce.

BLUE CHEESE SAUCE

¼ pound of any creamy blue cheese—Gorgonzola is excellent
⅔ cup sour cream
⅓ cup mayonnaise
1½ teaspoon Worcestershire sauce
1 teaspoon kosher salt
1 teaspoon pepper

Blend all in a food processor, or mash together in a large bowl. To use as salad dressing, thin with buttermilk.

FABULOUS FAJITAS

This is my favorite fajita recipe, in part because it's pretty basic without a lot of "fluffing up." Misc. notes—use skirt steak, not flank steak. A whole skirt steak is about 18-28 inch long, narrow and thin. Cut it in 4 manageable pieces to fit your skillet. Cook over high heat in two batches. Don't crowd the pan or the meat will steam instead of sear. You can also do this on the grill, but I think the results are better in a skillet.

1 skirt steak, about 1½ pounds, cut into four pieces.
Oil for cooking meat and vegetables
Salt and fresh ground black pepper
3-4 tablespoon ground cumin
1 tablespoon liquid smoke, but eliminate this if cooking on a grill
3 medium cloves of garlic, minced (or use a garlic press)
4 tablespoons lime juice (about 2 limes)
2 avocados (ripe—they have to be soft)
1-2 red onions, peeled and halved lengthwise, then cut each half into 6 wedges—it's easier if you leave the root end intact
1-2 red or green peppers, seeded and cut into 6 wedges
1 cup reduced fat sour cream, or regular if you prefer
12 large tortillas—I skip them, but you're supposed to wrap the fajitas in them.

Heat oven to lowest possible setting and put an ovenproof dish or pan in the oven. Heat a heavy bottomed 12-inch skillet on top the stove over medium low heat. Meanwhile, coat both sides of meat with just enough oil to get seasonings to stick. Sprinkle both sides with salt, pepper and some of the cumin, rubbing into the meat, and the liquid smoke if using. Set aside.

Mix garlic and 3 tablespoons lime juice in a shallow non-reactive baking pan—Pyrex, for instance. Set near the stove.

Peel the avocadoes and mash with the remaining lime juice (to taste—you may not want it all) to make a chunky guacamole. Set aside.

When ready to cook, turn heat up to medium high and turn on exhaust fan. When the skillet is *hot*, add the two thickest pieces of steak to the skillet. Sear on first side, about 3 minutes. Turn and cook to sear the other sides, 2-3 minutes for medium. Transfer to the dish with the lime-garlic marinade, turn to coat, and place in the dish in the warm oven. Cook remaining two thinner pieces of steak, about 2 minutes per side. Add to the marinade, turning to coat. Return to warm oven.

Pour off all but about 2 tablespoon of fat from the skillet. Add peppers and onions, sauté until crisp-tender, about 8 minutes.

Slice meat thinly, across the grain. Transfer to a platter with the peppers and onions; pour the lime marinade over the meat. Serve with the sour cream, avocadoes and tortillas. A little salsa wouldn't hurt either.

The fastest way to heat tortillas is in a plastic bag in the microwave—4 at a time, they take about 30 seconds.

BEEF STROGANOFF

There are lots of recipes for this dish. This is a classic version— except that those French chefs cooking for the Russian aristocracy would not have used "sour cream" as called for here, and which in this country is traditional—sour cream is an Americanism. They would have used crème fraîche, and you may find it interesting to try that instead; the result is a bit more subtle and I like it, but most American palates will miss the wham-bang of the sour cream. It is generally served today over noodles, but the original concept was to strew matchstick potatoes on top—and, though it smacks of decadence, I have been known to do both. Nothing succeeds like excess.

3 teaspoons powdered mustard
3 teaspoons sugar, separated
2 teaspoons salt
4-5 tablespoons oil
2 large or 3 medium onions, thinly sliced (about 4 cups)
1 pound mushrooms, thinly sliced lengthwise
2 pounds fillet of beef, trimmed of all fat (or use sirloin)
1 teaspoon fresh black pepper
1 jigger (1½ tablespoons) brandy or cognac
1 pint sour cream (or crème fraîche, see my notes above)
Optional: cooked noodles or crisply fried matchstick potatoes (see my notes above)

In small bowl, combine mustard, 1½ teaspoons sugar, pinch of salt and enough hot water, about a tablespoon, to form a thick paste. Let rest at room temperature about 15 minutes. Heat 2 tablespoons oil in heavy 10-12 inch skillet over high heat until a light haze forms.

Drop in onions and mushrooms, cover pan, and reduce heat to low. Simmer 20-30 minutes until soft, stirring occasionally. Drain in sieve, discard liquid, and return onions and mushrooms to skillet.

With sharp knife, cut fillet across the grain into ¼ inch rounds (this is easier if meat is partially frozen). Slice each round with the grain into ¼ inch strips. Heat 2 tablespoons oil in another heavy skillet over high heat until very hot but not smoking. Drop in half the meat and tossing constantly with large spoon, fry 2 minutes or until meat is lightly browned. Transfer meat to the vegetable skillet and fry remaining meat, add oil if necessary. When all meat is done, return to the skillet.

Heat the brandy slightly, pour over the meat, and ignite, being careful not to set the kitchen or your hair on fire. When the flames have died out, stir in remaining salt, pepper and the mustard paste. Stir in sour cream, a tablespoon at a time, then add remaining ½ teaspoon sugar and reduce heat to low. Cover pan and heat 2-3 minutes, just until sauce is heated through; do not boil. Taste for seasoning. To serve, transfer contents to heated serving platter or serve over noodles, and/ or scatter matchstick potatoes on top.

MARINATED TRI-TIPS

This is simply the best recipe I know for a tri-tip to cook on the grill, or you can do it in the oven. The funny thing is, the marinade being so simple, you would think you would taste the individual ingredients, but they blend so perfectly, you really aren't conscious of soy or beer or even all that garlic. Highly recommended.

1 tri-tip roast
1 cup soy sauce
1 bottle beer (any kind will do but a light colored lager style is best)
6-10 garlic cloves, peeled but left whole

Place the tri-tip in a Ziploc bag, add the remaining ingredients and marinate overnight. Grill to desired wellness, let rest 10 minutes, and cut against the grain.

BRAISED FAGGOTS (BRITISH MEATBALLS)

Okay, okay, but these would be tasty by any name.

¾ pound ground beef
½ pound ground pork
1 medium onion (about 4-5 ounces) finely chopped
1 carrot, peeled and finely chopped
1 celery stalk, finely chopped
1-2 tablespoons finely chopped parsley
1 tablespoon tomato paste
1-2 garlic cloves, crushed
About 3 ounces dry breadcrumbs
2 eggs
Salt and pepper
Pinch of sage
Pinch of thyme
6 tablespoons butter
6 tablespoons flour
4 cups beef broth

Preheat oven to 350°. Combine first 13 ingredients (beef through thyme) and mix well; shape into balls the size and shape of large eggs and place in deep baking dish.

Melt butter in saucepan, add flour, cook a few minutes, stirring, and add broth. Bring to simmer and cook, stirring, until thickened. Pour over meatballs, cover with lid or foil, and bake for 1½-2 hours.

BRAISED BRISKET OF BEEF

This is the recipe, more or less, from Junior's, the famous deli in Brooklyn, where they sell tons of it. By the way, if you like New York style cheesecake, they are famous for that, too, and though I don't have that recipe to give you, you can order it online, and I can't imagine you could get a better one. There is a funny story about a fire at the deli, and the customers were all herded outside, where they proceeded to chant to the firemen, "Save the cheesecake, save the cheesecake...". And this brisket is fabulous, too.

About 2 lbs beef brisket—*not corned*
1-2 onions, cut up roughly in chunks
1-2 carrots, the same

1 or 2 stalks of celery, ditto
2 tablespoons molasses, the dark stuff
Salt and pepper
2 cups beef stock

Put vegetables in roasting pan, set beef on top of them, pour the stock over and around—be sure the stock comes about half way up the sides of the beef; add more stock if necessary. Salt and pepper, then spread the molasses on the top surface of the beef.

Cover pan tightly. Bring the liquid to a simmer on top of stove (if your baking dish is not safe for stovetop cooking, heat the stock to a boil separately and pour over the meat), then transfer to a 325° oven, cook 3-4 hours, till fork tender. Let rest 10-15 minutes. Slice across the grain. Serve with gravy or (my preference) some of the strained cooking liquid and some horseradish.

RED WINE BRAISED BEEF BRISKET

Zinfandel is perfect for this and an ideal accompaniment to serve with it, but any dry, fruity wine, such as a Beaujolais, will work.

2 cups red wine (see note, above)
½ cup chicken broth (I use the fat-free reduced sodium version, but hey, it's your arteries)
¼ cup tomato paste
2½ pound brisket, trimmed (the butcher has probably already done that)
2 teaspoons salt
½ teaspoon freshly ground black pepper
Cooking spray
8 cups sliced sweet onions (Vidalia, *e.g.*, or Walla Walla) about 4 medium onions
2 tablespoons sugar
1¼ teaspoons dried thyme
6 cloves of garlic, thinly sliced
2 carrots, peeled and cut in ½ inch slices
2 celery stacks, cut in ½ inch slices
1½ pounds small red potatoes, cut in quarters
1½ teaspoons extra virgin olive oil
1 teaspoon dried oregano
¼ teaspoon ground red (cayenne) pepper
Chopped parsley

Heat the oven to 325°. Whisk together the wine, chicken broth and tomato paste.

Heat a large Dutch oven over medium high heat. Season the beef with about ¾ teaspoon of salt and ¼ teaspoon of the pepper. Coat the pan with cooking spray (now, if you don't care about the cholesterol and the fat, you can just heat some oil in the pan and use that instead of the cooking spray—I'm trying to keep you alive long enough to finish the book). Brown the beef on all sides (remember the princess—forget all that silliness you read in other cookbooks about doing this to "seal" the meat. It doesn't. It just adds flavor. Do the top and the bottom and forget trying to stand it on its sides, as I've seen some cooks do) for about 8 minutes, and remove it to a platter, and cover to keep warm.

Add the onions to the pan, and ½ teaspoon salt, ¼ teaspoon pepper, the sugar and 1 teaspoon of the thyme. Cook until the onions are tender and golden brown, stirring occasionally, about 20 minutes in all. Toss in the garlic, the celery and the carrots and cook another 5 minutes, stirring occasionally. Place the beef on top of the onions, pour the wine over all, cover, and place in the oven. Bake for 1¾ hours.

Meanwhile, place the potatoes in a large bowl and sprinkle with ¾ teaspoons salt, ¼ teaspoon thyme, the olive oil, oregano, and red pepper, and toss to coat all.

After the 1¾ hours, remove beef from the oven and turn over. Place seasoned potatoes in a baking dish on the lower rack in the oven. Cover the beef and return it the oven. Bake 45 minutes or until the beef is tender.

Remove the beef from the oven, cover it to keep warm. Raise the oven temperature to 425°, and move the potatoes to the middle rack, bake for 15 minutes or until crisp and edges have browned.

Remove the beef from the pan, cut in thin slices across the grain. Serve with the onion mixture and the potatoes, sprinkled with parsley. Makes about 8 servings.

BISTECCA ALLA FIORENTINA

This can be done with veal T-bone steaks also. I prefer the skillet method

4 T-bone steaks, 1½ inches thick
¼ cup olive oil
¼ teaspoon minced garlic
4 teaspoons salt

1 teaspoons ground black pepper
2 teaspoons minced rosemary leaves
3 tablespoons lemon juice

Prepare grill to hot on one side, with no coals on the other half. Brush steaks with some of the oil and season generously with garlic, salt, pepper and rosemary.

Grill over direct heat about 2 minutes each side, until marked, move to the cooler side of the grill and continue to grill over indirect heat, 5-6 minutes per side. Transfer the meat to a cutting board or large platter. Drizzle each with 2 teaspoons more of the oil and sprinkle with lemon juice.

You can do one or two steaks in a heavy (preferably cast iron) ungreased skillet, heated to very hot. Sear for 2 minutes on each side, reduce heat and continue till desired doneness—or place skillet in a preheated 350° oven to finish cooking.

DEVILED ROAST BEEF SLICES

A great way to use leftover roast beef. I like this well enough that I always plan a large enough roast to have left over slices. Why the devil they are called deviled, though, I don't know

Slice leftover beef rather thickly. Beat 2 eggs until light and foamy and pour into a shallow dish. Pour dried breadcrumbs, plain or seasoned, into another dish. Heat butter or half butter and half oil in a skillet, dip the slices into the egg and then the crumbs, and sauté until the crumbs are crusty and brown. Serve with Brown Sauce or Sauce Diable (see sauces), or the gravy from Leftover Beef Yorkshire.

GRILLED FLANK STEAK WITH
RED WINE/SHALLOT SAUCE

Brush flank steak with soy sauce, sprinkle well with salt, pepper, and 1 teaspoon dried crumbled thyme. Let stand for an hour or so, brush again with soy and grill over a brisk fire, 3-4 minutes per side for rare. Remove from grill and keep warm. For sauce: combine 1½ cups chopped shallots or green onions and 1½ cups red wine. Bring just to boiling point. Add 1 stick butter and salt to taste, stir until butter is melted. Add 2 tablespoons finely chopped parsley and spoon over sliced steak.

VICTOR'S PARTY MEAT LOAF

This is good hot or cold, and it makes a terrific main course for a buffet. Sometimes I make the loaves long and slender and serve it as a country style pâté, sliced thin and garnished with cornichons and little pickled onions. You can add some lemon juice and a dash of Worcestershire sauce to some mayonnaise and serve that with it.

2 pounds ground beef
1 pound ground pork
2 garlic cloves, finely chopped
1 fairly large onion, chopped finely
1 teaspoon salt
1 teaspoon ground black pepper
1 crumbled bay leaf
½ teaspoon crumbled thyme leaves
1 teaspoon freshly chopped green pepper
½ cup dry breadcrumbs
2 eggs
Bacon or salt pork

Mix all ingredients except bacon and knead with the fingers until very thoroughly blended. Form into a long loaf or cake and press firmly. Arrange enough slices of bacon or salt pork on the bottom of a baking pan to hold the meat loaf and set the meat loaf on the bacon. Brush the loaf with butter and cross the top with 2-4 additional slices of bacon. Roast at 325°, basting occasionally, for 1½-1¾ hours, or until cooked through. Constant basting makes a moister loaf. If you serve hot, allow to stand on a hot platter 10-15 minutes before you slice it.

BŒUF À LA MODE EN GELÉE

This is the dish you want for your grandest Christmas buffet. It takes time and is a bit of work, and you need room in your refrigerator for a large platter, but it is guaranteed to impress even your most sophisticated foodie friends. This is intended to be served cold (en gelée means in aspic) but it is also good warm, with some of the juices spooned over it. For that buffet, though, it is awfully pretty in the aspic.

4-5 pound pot roast, boned and tied (shoulder or chuck)
2 tablespoons butter
2 thin slices salt pork, diced, or substitute bacon.
1 onion sliced
¼ cup brandy
1 carrot, sliced
1 teaspoon thyme
1 bay leaf
2 springs parsley
1 teaspoon salt
½ teaspoon pepper
1 cup water
1 cup dry white wine
Aspic glaze (see below)
For garnish: cooked carrots, drained; boiled small white onions, drained; green onion tops, blanched and drained.

Melt butter in Dutch oven add meat and brown lightly on all sides. Add salt pork and sliced onions and brown meat well. Add brandy, ignite (if you have a cabinet right over the stove, be prepared to quickly whisk the pot away until the fire dies, or you may set things on fire. I burned up an exhaust fan one time) and when flames die, add sliced carrot, thyme, bay leaf, parsley, salt, pepper, water and wine. Cover, bring to a boil, then reduce heat and simmer 3-4 hours or until meat is fork tender but still holds it shape. Let meat rest before carving.

To serve *en gelée*, drain meat and chill thoroughly. You can use the liquid for other purposes, or some of it for the aspic, see below. Prepare aspic. Slice well-chilled meat thin, taking pains to cut even slices. Place in a deep platter, slices slightly overlapping, and rows even for best effect. Pour about ¾ cup of the slightly thickened aspic glaze over meat to anchor it in place and give it a shiny surface; then add decorations. Slice carrots into diagonals and carefully press slices in a flower petal design into the semi-firm glaze. Add onions as flower centers and bits of green onion, blanched to make flexible, as leaves, stems, etc. Chill all until glaze is firm, keeping remaining glaze chilled but not set, so it can still be poured. Pour more glaze over meat and chill until glaze is set and the decorations are firmly anchored; if necessary, repeat, until you have a gleaming layer of aspic overall, chilling the platter in the refrigerator with each application. Pour any remaining glaze into a small, shallow pan and chill until firm. Cut into squares or diamonds or chop with a knife, and spoon it around edge of platter, over any glitches, etc. Keep chilled until time to serve.

ASPIC GLAZE

1 envelope Knox unflavored gelatin
½ cup cold water
2 (10½ ounce) cans consommé (or use 1 can and about 1¼ cups of the cooking liquid, strained, chilled and all fat removed.
1 teaspoon Lemon juice

Soften gelatin in cold water. Combine consommé and gelatin in a saucepan and bring to boil, stirring to dissolve gelatin. Remove from heat, add lemon juice and chill until slightly thickened. Use as above.

BRAISED SHORT RIBS WITH ROSEMARY AND GARLIC

2 pounds beef short ribs, bone in
Salt and pepper
1 tablespoon or more of oil or butter
2 cups chopped onion
2 ribs of celery, chopped
½ pound carrots, chopped
6 cloves garlic, smashed or pressed
2 sprigs fresh rosemary
1½ cups chicken stock
1 cup red wine

Preheat oven to 325°. Preheat over high heat a large, deep pan that can hold the ribs in one layer. Dry the ribs with paper towels, sprinkle generously with salt and pepper. Add the oil to the pan, and sear the ribs until well browned on all sides, turning periodically to brown evenly. Remove the ribs to a plate, pour off and discard all but 1 tablespoon of fat, reduce heat to medium and cook the vegetables until they begin to brown lightly, about 10 minutes. Return the ribs to the pan with any accumulated juices, add the rosemary, stock and wine, bring to a boil, turn the heat off, cover the pan, and place in the oven. Bake 45 minutes, turn the ribs, cover again, and bake 45 minutes. Strain the cooking liquid and discard solids. Skim extra fat (or chill overnight and remove the fat), then cook the liquid down a bit until it gets glossy, and add the ribs to reheat.

►*Veal and Lamb*

ROSEMARY VEAL STEW

This is a favorite; it tastes good, but also, low in carbs, it's good for the diabetic. I sometimes cut a piece of puff pastry into the size and shape of my serving dish and bake it separately according to the package directions. I pour the stew into the serving dish, and set the crust on top. This qualifies as en crouté, *which just means covered in pastry. It makes a beautiful presentation for a dressy dinner. You could, by the way, actually bake it with the pastry covering, but your vegetables will almost certainly be overcooked.*

1¼ pounds veal cubes (tell the butcher you want stew meat)
1 tablespoon all purpose flour
1 tablespoon oil
1 cup chopped onion
2 cloves garlic, minced
1 cup water
1 cup sliced carrots
⅓ cup chopped parsley
½ teaspoon dried rosemary, crumbled
¼ teaspoon ground black pepper
½-¾ pounds green beans, trimmed (2-3 cups)
Salt to taste
Optional: 12 small white or brown mushrooms, trimmed and halved

Dredge veal in flour. Heat oil over high heat in large nonstick pot. Add veal and brown, about 5-7 minutes. Add onion and garlic and stir about 1 minute, until slightly softened. Add water, bring to boil. Cover, reduce heat and simmer 45 minutes, until the meat is tender. Add carrots, parsley, rosemary and pepper. Simmer covered 10 minutes.

Add green beans, and mushrooms, if using; simmer covered 7 minutes or until beans are of desired doneness. Taste for salt.

Vitello Tonnato (Veal in Tuna Sauce)

This is another of those old-fashioned dishes one doesn't see much anymore, and that is really too bad, because this is both superb and a unique blending of flavors, like nothing else I know of. It is worthy of centering your most special warm weather buffet, or it could be an appetizer, or a luncheon, or supper on a hot, languid day, served with nothing more than some cold, parsleyed rice, sliced tomatoes, a nice, dry white Italian wine, and some fruit and cheese. It's a bit of work, but all can be done ahead; really, must be, so the delicate veal can soak up the sauce's robust flavor.

3-4 pound leg of veal (or shoulder, but not breast), boned, rolled and
    tied—by all means, have your butcher do this
1 (2-ounce) can flat filets of anchovies (needless to say, the best you
    can find)
2 whole cloves
2 medium onions
2 carrots, peeled and quartered
2 stalks of celery, keep the leaves attached
2 bay leaves
3 parsley sprigs
1 cup dry vermouth)
2 tablespoons salt
¼ teaspoon freshly ground black pepper
6 tablespoons lemon juice (about 3 lemons)
Water
2 (6½-7 ounce) cans of tuna, the best you can find
2 cups mayonnaise
2 tablespoons capers, drained (salt packed are best, if you can find
    them; soak them a bit in water, say 30 minutes, and then drain;
    but the ones in brine, drained, will do)

Cut four of the anchovies in half. Make 8 slits in the veal roast, and insert the anchovies in the slits. Stick a whole clove in each onion. Place the meat, vegetables, bay leaves and parsley in a Dutch oven or large kettle. Add the wine, salt, pepper, 4 tablespoons of the lemon juice, and enough water just to cover the meat. Cover the pot, bring to a boil, reduce heat and simmer gently 1½ hours or until tender. Cool the meat completely in the broth.

    Remove the cooled meat from the broth and set meat aside. Strain the broth and set it aside. Put the tuna and the remaining anchovies in the food processor and combine—or pound them in a bowl to mince or purée. Or you can put them on a good solid plate and smoosh them around with the bottom of a flat-bottomed glass or ramekin.

Combine tuna mixture, 2 tablespoons lemon juice, mayonnaise, capers and ½ cup of the reserved cooking stock. Mix thoroughly, taste, and season with salt and pepper.

Remove the strings from the veal, pat the meat dry with paper towels, and slice thinly. Reassemble on a large serving dish and pour the sauce around the meat (or, alternatively, fan out the slices neatly, glaze them with some of the sauce and spoon the rest around them) Cover and refrigerate at least 1 and up to 2 days. Garnish with lemon slices and parsley.

BRAISED VEAL SHANKS WITH SAUSAGES AND TOMATOES (RONCHYS DE VEAU)

This is a French variation of the Italian ossi buchi. Serve it with rice and Parmesan cheese to sprinkle on top. You can skip the sausages, but they add an interesting element. A purée of celery root and potato would be a good substitute for the rice, and a salad of endive and julienne beets would be a good go-along. Veal shanks are not always to be found, but your butcher can certainly order them for you.

12 pieces veal shank, cut 2-2½ inches long (have your butcher do this)
Salt and pepper
3 tablespoons butter
2 tablespoons oil
6 very large ripe tomatoes, peeled, halved and seeded
2 cups dry vermouth
½ cup chopped parsley
1½ teaspoons dried basil
3 tablespoons tomato paste
24 small pork sausages

Season the veal with salt and pepper, combine the butter and oil in a large pan and sauté the veal until nicely browned. Stand the shanks upright in a Dutch oven or large kettle, top each one with half of a tomato, and pour the white wine all around. Cover and simmer for ten minutes, add the parsley and basil, cover again, and simmer over very low heat for 1 hour. Add the tomato paste, and simmer for another ½-1 hour, until the meat is very tender. Meanwhile, poach the sausages in water to cover, cold to start, and when it comes to the boil, reduce heat and simmer 5 minutes; drain. Add to the veal shanks for the last ten minutes cooking time.

EMINCÉ DE VEAU (MINCED VEAL WITH CREAM)

Despite its name, the veal in this dish is not chopped, but cut into strips. It is a quick dish, for when you want something nice but don't have a lot of time. You can buy the veal the day before, for instance, cut it into strips and refrigerate, and you can clarify the butter ahead as well, so it will take you literally minutes to cook them. Serve with roasted potatoes, or rice, or noodles.

1-pound boneless veal cutlets, cut in 1-inch wide strips, about 2
    inches long
Flour for dredging
4 tablespoons clarified butter*
Salt and pepper
¼ cup dry white wine
⅔ cup cream

Dredge the veal strips in flour, shake off excess, and sauté in the butter over medium high heat, until just cooked through, about 2-3 minutes, with a stir or two along the way. Season with salt and pepper and remove the meat to a hot serving dish. Add wine to the pan and deglaze over high heat, stirring up any brown bits, or "fond," stir in the cream and cook down for 1-2 minutes. You can use sour cream, but be sure not to let it boil. Return veal to the pan just to heat through, and serve immediately.

*Note: to clarify butter, melt and let it sit to cool, but not firm up. The milky white solids will settle at the bottom of your container. The clear liquid at the top is the clarified butter. Pour it off carefully. The leavings can be added to a sauce. You can also sometimes find ghee in markets, which will work as well.

VEAL SCALLOPS

Veal scallops are probably the most popular cut of veal, and certainly the most versatile. Quick to cook, you can have an easy dinner with rice, noodles, potatoes, or just a green vegetable or a salad.

There is not much to cooking them, Heat butter and oil, about half and half, over medium high heat, in a skillet (if you are cooking for several and are dexterous, you may want to use 2 skillets, so they will all be done about the same time) till the butter stops foaming. Flour the scallops lightly, shake off any excess, and sauté quickly, about 1-2 minutes, no more, to a side, until lightly browned, season with salt and pepper, and then proceed in one of the following manners:

VEAL SCALLOPS PICCATA

Pour ¼ cup lemon juice, 8-10 thin slices of lemon, and 1 tablespoons chopped Italian parsley into the pan with the scallops, swirl about quickly, remove scallops to a hot platter or dinner plate, and pour sauce over.

VEAL SCALLOPS WITH SHERRY OR MARSALA

Remove the scallops from the pan first, then deglaze the pan with ⅔ cup oloroso sherry or Marsala (or you can use tawny port).

VEAL SCALLOPS WITH CREAM

Remove the scallops; pour ⅔ cup heavy cream into the skillet and cook down 2 to 3 minutes.

You can pound chicken or turkey cutlets thin and cook in any of the above ways. The best way to pound them is to put them individually into the plastic bags from your supermarket produce section. Save those bags in an empty Kleenex box.

LAMB CHOPS DIJONNAISE

Anything Dijonnaise is made with Dijon mustard, of course. French food titles are a kind of shorthand: Lyonnaise means potatoes and Soubise means onions, and Florentine means spinach—you can go on and on.

Marinade:
2 tablespoon Dijon mustard
1 tablespoon minced garlic
2 teaspoons fresh minced rosemary leaves

½ teaspoon ground pepper
1 teaspoon olive oil
1 teaspoon dry vermouth

4 double lamb rib chops
Kosher salt
1 cup Italian seasoned dry bread crumbs
Oil for browning

Mix marinade ingredients together, spread over chops. Marinate 2 hours. Preheat oven to 400°. With paper towels, wipe most of the marinade off chops, leaving a thin coating. Season with salt and pepper and coat with breadcrumbs. Heat a large ovenproof skillet over medium high heat, coat lightly with oil. When oil shimmers, place chops carefully into skillet and brown crust on both sides, then place skillet in oven to finish cooking, about 15 minutes. Serve plain or with optional sauce.

Optional sauce:
½ cup minced yellow onion
1 tablespoon unsalted butter
1 cup red wine
1½ cups low salt beef stock
1 teaspoon Dijon mustard
¼ teaspoon minced rosemary
¼ teaspoon minced thyme
2 tablespoons heavy cream.
2 tablespoons butter, cut into pieces

Before browning the chops, sweat onion in 1 tablespoon butter in a small saucepan over medium high heat, covered, until soft, just a minute or two. Add red wine and cook until almost dry. Stir in well the beef stock and Dijon. Stir in minced rosemary and minced thyme, then immediately strain the broth. Return to pan and set aside. Just before serving, bring to simmer and add heavy cream, Cook for 3-4 minutes, then swirl in 2 tablespoons butter, a piece at a time. Taste and adjust seasoning.

VICTOR'S LAMB CHOPS

Season lamb chops with salt and pepper, flour lightly and fry in clarified butter till well browned on both sides. Add 1 tablespoon brandy, 6 tablespoons heavy cream, 6 tablespoons chicken stock (or half chicken stock, half beef), 2 fresh sage leaves. Cover, simmer gently for 20 minutes. Remove chops, add ½ tablespoon lemon juice to pan and adjust seasoning. Reduce slightly if sauce seems thin.

LEG OF LAMB

A leg of lamb is a lovely dish for a festive occasion, and happily once it is in the oven, needs no attention beyond checking the temperature to be sure it doesn't overcook. A good lamb leg should never be cooked beyond medium rare (125-130° on a meat thermometer). If you object to pink meat, the alternative is what is sometimes called Spoon Leg of Lamb, and I will include that recipe after this one.

5-6 pound leg of lamb
6 cloves of garlic, pressed
2 tablespoons olive oil
1 teaspoon crumbled dried rosemary
Salt and freshly ground pepper
Optional: 1 tablespoon Dijon mustard

Combine everything but the lamb, rub the lamb all over with the mixture, and let it sit for 30 minutes to one hour. Heat the oven to 350°, and roast on a rack in a shallow pan for about 1-1½ hours, testing the temperature after the first hour. If you have a well-insulated oven (preferably self cleaning), you can start the lamb at 450° degrees for 25 minutes, and then reduce the heat to 350°, which will give you a crustier exterior. In that case, check your temperature after 45 minutes.

GIGOT DE SEPT HEURES (SEVEN-HOUR LAMB)

*The funny English name for this dish, **Spoon Leg of Lamb**, just means that when it is done it is so soft that it can almost be eaten with a spoon. This goes very well with white beans (canellini). The canned ones are excellent, just rinse under running water and drain, and heat with some garlic, salt and pepper, and a little basil, or some minced anchovy. There are several steps to this lamb, but they are done way before you want to serve it, and after that, the little lamb takes care of itself, Bo Peep, until serving time.*

5-6 pound leg of lamb, boned and tied (ask your butcher to saw the
   bones into small pieces for you and take them home too)
Salt and pepper
3 medium onions, each stuck with 2 whole cloves
3 carrots, halved lengthwise
6 cloves of garlic
½ cup olive oil
1 teaspoon dried thyme
1 bay leaf
1 sprig parsley
4 ripe tomatoes, peeled, seeded and coarsely chopped
1 cup red wine
Parsley for garnish

Preheat oven to 400°. Rub the leg with salt and pepper, place on a
rack in a large roasting pan, and add the bones, the onions, the carrots, and 4 cloves of the garlic to the pan. Pour the oil over the vegetables and the bones, and roast for 30 minutes. Lower the heat to
350° and roast 30 minutes more. Remove the pan from the oven and
reduce the oven temperature to 200°.

   Transfer the lamb to a large casserole or baking dish, add the
vegetables, bones and any cooking juices from the roasting pan, plus
the remaining 2 cloves of garlic, 1 teaspoon each of salt and pepper,
the thyme, bay leaf, parsley and tomatoes. Rinse the roasting pan
with the red wine and pour that over the meat. Cover the baking dish
tightly (if your lid is not heavy and tight-fitting, cover first with foil,
then the lid), return to the oven, and cook for 6 hours, by which time
the meat should be tender indeed (I suspect this could be done in a
slow cooker, at the slowest setting, but I have never tried that.)

   Remove the meat to a hot platter and remove the strings. Discard the bones and the bay leave, remove the cloves from the onions
and skim excess fat from the pan. You can serve the cooking juices
and vegetables as they are, or purée them all to make a sauce, or
strain and degrease the juices and serve them alone. Garnish with
parsley.

▶ *Vegetables and Sides*

GRATIN DAUPHINOIS

This is to die for—and if you have it very often, you might. Still, far be it from me to deny myself—or anyone else—the pleasure. The exact measurements don't matter much; I have done this with one potato in a small baking dish. Don't drown the potatoes with the milk/cream mixture. That should come to about a half inch of the top. Check the potatoes about halfway through the cooking time, and if the liquid looks excessive, spoon some of it out, and reserve it, in case you need it later.

Preheat oven to 400°. Butter a large baking dish with 1 tablespoon butter and scatter 1 minced garlic clove over the bottom. Cut 6 large russet potatoes in thin slices and arrange in slightly overlapping layers; season each layer with salt, pepper and freshly grated nutmeg. Spread 1 cup crème fraîche over the potatoes. Heat 2 cups milk and 2 cups heavy cream to a boil, pour over the potatoes. Dot with 3 tablespoons butter cut into bits. Bake about 1-1½ hours, until brown and bubbling and the potatoes are tender.

HASH BROWN CASSEROLE

Sort of like Cracker Barrel's.

2 tablespoons butter
½ cup chopped onion
1 can Cheddar Cheese soup
½ cup milk
4 shakes Tabasco
1 package frozen shredded hash browns
2 cups shredded cheddar cheese

Preheat oven to 350°. Coat a 13 x 9 baking dish with cooking spray.

In a 2-quart saucepan, melt butter over medium heat and cook onion, stirring, until soft, 3-4 minutes. Add soup, milk, and Tabasco, stir to blend and heat through. Place potatoes in a large bowl. Add soup mixture and 1½ cups of the cheese, stir to blend, turn into prepared baking dish. Sprinkle remaining cheese on top and bake until bubbling and golden, 30 minutes.

POTATOES IN BEER

Good with steaks, chops, poultry. Less fattening than the usual scalloped potatoes. Men folk generally love these. Allow plenty of time, they can sometimes be slow (I mean the potatoes, not the men—well, yes...oh, never mind), but they can be kept warm while you finish other projects. Easier done with potatoes than men.

3 pounds potatoes, peeled and thinly sliced
1 large onion, thinly sliced
¼ cup flour
1½ cups (about 6 ounces) grated Swiss cheese
Salt and pepper
1½ cups beer

Preheat oven to 400° and generously butter 2½ to 3-quart casserole. Cover bottom of casserole with ⅓ of the potatoes, spread with half the onions and sprinkle with 2 tablespoon flour, then ½ cup cheese, then salt and pepper generously. Repeat layers, using half the remaining potatoes, all the remaining onion, all the remaining flour and ½ cup more of cheese. Salt and pepper. Spread remaining potatoes on top and sprinkle with the last ½ cup of cheese. Pour in the beer—it should come about ½ way up the potatoes. Bake for 1-1½ hours, until well browned and fork tender (some potatoes take longer than others). Check from time to time to make sure they are not drying out, and add more beer if necessary, but don't flood them. Serves 4-6.

BLUE CHEESE AND ROSEMARY SCALLOPED POTATOES

These are so fabulous, but hell on diabetic diets. They are better served fresh from the oven but they can also be made in advance and kept warm, or covered and refrigerated for up to 2 days. Bring to room temperature and reheat at 350° till hot. If they seem too dry, add a little extra cream when reheating.

5 pounds Russet potatoes
2 teaspoons salt
½ teaspoon freshly ground black pepper
1½ teaspoon minced fresh rosemary leaves
¾ cup crumbled blue cheese
¾ cup grated Parmesan cheese
1 cup sour cream
2 cups heavy cream
1 teaspoon salt

Preheat oven to 350°, butter a 9 x 13 glass-baking dish. Peel and slice the potatoes in ¼ inch slices. Toss them in large bowl with salt, pepper and rosemary.

In a small bowl, toss cheeses together.

Layer half the potatoes in the buttered baking dish, sprinkle with half the cheese mixture and top with remaining potatoes. In bowl, whisk together sour cream, heavy cream and 1-teaspoon salt. Pour over potatoes. Rap the baking dish on the counter to spread out sauce and help release any air bubbles. Sprinkle with remaining cheese mixture. Bake for about 1 hour and 15 minutes, or until browned and completely tender all the way through when stabbed with a knife.

PROSCIUTTO AND GRUYÈRE BAKED POTATOES

Truly addictive, a wonderful go-along for a roast, or if you use large potatoes, sufficient unto themselves for a luncheon or brunch dish. You can bake them and serve them immediately, or do everything but the final browning, and finish them just before eating, or even wrap them in non-stick foil, freeze, and have them later.

4 medium large baking (*e.g.*, Idaho) potatoes
2 teaspoons olive oil
1½ cups (about 6 ounces) shredded Gruyère or other Swiss cheese
⅔ cup (about 3 ounces) chopped prosciutto
½ cup whipping cream, hot
2 tablespoons butter, softened
½ teaspoon salt
¼ teaspoon freshly ground pepper
¼ teaspoon freshly grated nutmeg

Preheat oven to 400°. With a fork, pierce the skins of the potatoes in several places, rub them with the olive oil, and bake them about 1 hour, until tender.

Cut the potatoes in half lengthwise while hot, and scoop the flesh into a large bowl, leaving just enough flesh in the skins to make the shells firm enough to hold the filling. Mash the potato flesh until smooth, or process through a ricer. Add one cup of the grated cheese, and the prosciutto and stir. Add the hot cream and the butter, stir again until well mixed, and stir in salt, pepper and nutmeg

Fill the potato shells with the mixture and top with the remaining ½ cup of cheese. You can make the potatoes ahead to this point and keep at room temperature for up to 2 hours, loosely covered, or 1 day in the refrigerator, or they can be wrapped in Non-stick aluminum foil and frozen.

When you are ready to bake them, place on a baking sheet and bake 20-30 minutes until hot and the cheese is golden brown. If you are baking them from frozen, allow about 45 minutes

VICTOR'S POTATO SALAD

Over the years, my potato salad has earned many fans, including some who insisted beforehand that they did not like potato salad. I am often asked for the recipe. The difficulty is, there isn't a recipe, it's more of a plot outline. Here is what I do:

I combine, about half and half, baking potatoes, such as Idahoes, which soak up the dressings better but tend to crumble, and the waxy boiling potatoes, the white or red or yellow ones, which hold together better but don't absorb as well. As a rule of thumb, about 1 potato for each serving, but of course if they are huge, half a potato will suffice. I halve them and boil them in salted water in the skins until fork tender, but not falling apart, and peel them and slice them thickly while they are still hot. If I am in a hurry, I peel them and slice them thickly before cooking them, and boil the slices, which takes much less time, but you must be extra careful not to end up with mashed potatoes, and you lose a bit of flavor.

While the slices are still warm, I toss them with salt and pepper and a tablespoon or two of chopped shallots or scallions, and either (a tablespoon or two of dry vermouth or white wine vinegar, and a tablespoon two of chicken or beef stock, depending upon what I plan to serve this with) or (2-3 tablespoons of bottled vinaigrette—I like Girard's champagne dressing). I let the potatoes sit for 20 minutes or so, to soak all this up, then I add some chopped celery and 3-4 hard-boiled eggs, roughly chopped up (but save some of the prettiest slices for garnish). Finally, I toss everything with some sour cream and some mayonnaise, about ⅓ of the former to ⅔ of the latter, enough to bind everything together nicely.

Then I refrigerate it for an hour or so, or even overnight, since the potatoes and eggs may soak up quite a bit of the mayo, and you may need to add a little more. Finally, I lay some nice slices of hard boiled egg on top, and sprinkle all with a little finely chopped parsley, or alternatively, some rounds cut from the green end of some scallions, and either paprika or a very light dusting of cayenne, or even Old Bay.

This has a bit more flavor than most potato salads (without the mustard or the sweetening, both of which I dislike) and the inclusion of the sour cream makes it especially creamy.

I don't think it needs anything added, but once, for fun, I stirred in some frozen peas, and another time, some chopped pimento, and both were good.

TOMATOES À LA CRÈME

Core the stem end of six tomatoes and cut in half. Melt a lump of butter in a fry pan and put in tomatoes, cut side down. Puncture the skin (round) side of the tomatoes two or three times with the point of a sharp knife. Cook over medium heat for five minutes. Turn over, sprinkle with salt and cook for 10 minutes. Turn again, for 2-3 minutes, until the juices run out into the pan. Turn again, cut side up, and pour about 3 ounces of heavy cream into the pan, and mix with the juices. As soon as it bubbles, slip all into a hot dish and serve at once, ideally with some crusty bread. Messy, but good.

OVEN-ROASTED TOMATOES

Obviously you want the best tomatoes you can find. In San Francisco that means Muir Glen. San Marzanos are nice too. On toast, these make a terrific hors d'oeuvre.

Preheat oven to 275°. Pour ¼ cup extra virgin olive oil in a large non-reactive baking pan (glass or enameled). Add 1 chopped peeled small yellow onion, 2 thinly sliced (or minced) cloves garlic, 1 tablespoon fresh rosemary leaves and 3 tablespoons fresh parsley. Toss, then spread evenly on bottom of pan. Drain 2 28-ounce cans peeled whole tomatoes. Gently squeeze tomatoes to release excess juice, then place in pan in a single layer. Drizzle with ¼ cup olive oil, sprinkle with 1 teaspoon sugar, and season with salt and pepper. Bake for 3 hours. Serve hot or room temperature on grilled or toasted bread as antipasto or toss with pasta.

TWICE-COOKED BEETS IN GLAZE

Beets are the poor stepsisters at the vegetable ball, but they can be delicious, as in this somewhat unusual version.

8 2½-inch diameter beets, trimmed and scrubbed
4 tablespoons extra virgin olive oil
2 medium leaks, white and pale green parts only, trimmed, halved
    lengthwise, and thinly sliced, about 3 cups, and thoroughly
    rinsed—leeks can be gritty
2 cups Chianti or other dry red wine
2 tablespoons butter

Heat oven to 450º. Toss beets with 2 tablespoons oil in 13 x 9-inch glass baking dish, roast uncovered until tender when pierced with knife, about 1 hour. Cool slightly, slip off skins, cut into quarters. You can do that part ahead. Heat remaining 2 tablespoons oil in heavy large skillet over medium heat. Add leeks and sauté until translucent and tender, about 12 minutes. Add beets, sprinkle with salt and pepper, and sauté 5 minutes. Add Chianti and bring to boil, reduce heat to medium and simmer until most of the wine evaporates and glazes beets, stirring occasionally, about 15 minutes. Add butter and stir until melted. Season with salt and pepper

FANNY'S BROCCOLI AND RICE CASSEROLE

When my old home town recently celebrated its bicentennial, my sister, Fanny Kisling, wrote a series of articles for the local paper on the history of Eaton and the state of Ohio in general, going all the way back to Colonial times, and the articles were so enthusiastically received that readers literally demanded they be reissued in book form. Knowing Fan, I expected the book to be erudite, but happily, it also made for a couple of hours of delicious reading. Good job, Sis. I am happy to say, she is as good a cook as she is a writer, as evidenced by this recipe, and you will find it delicious too.

1 small onion, chopped
½ cup chopped celery
1 package frozen chopped broccoli, thawed
1 tablespoon butter
1 (8-ounce) jar processed cheese spread
1 can cream of mushroom soup
1 (5-ounce) can evaporated milk
3 cups cooked rice

In large skillet over medium heat, sauté onion, celery and broccoli in butter 3-5 minutes. Stir in cheese, soup, and evaporated milk, until smooth. Place rice in greased 8-inch baking dish, pour cheese mixture over top—do not stir. Bake uncovered at 325° for 25-30 minutes.

SAVORY WILD RICE

6 strips bacon, fried and crumbled
3 cups boiling water
1 cup wild rice
6 chopped scallions
1 stick butter, melted
½ cup grated Parmesan

Wash the rice, add with onion to boiling water, and simmer over low heat until water is absorbed, about 35 minutes. Mix in melted butter and Parmesan. Just before serving, mix in about half of the bacon and sprinkle the rest on top.

RICE SOUBISE

A beautiful accompaniment to a good roast of beef, roast chicken or leg of lamb. I have even served this with hamburger steaks, but the side dish does tend to outshine the main one in that case.

1½-2 cups chopped onions
2 tablespoons olive oil or other oil
¾ cup white long grain rice
¼ cup dry vermouth
1⅓ cups hot water
½-1 teaspoon salt, to taste
1 small bay leaf

½ cup heavy cream
½ cup grated Parmesan

In a 2-quart sauce pan with a heavy bottom, cook onions in oil, covered but stir from time to time, for about 20 minutes. The onions should be tender but not browned. Add rice and stir for 3-4 minutes, until rice turns from milky to translucent and back to milky. Add wine and hot water, salt and bay leaf, bring to simmer, and stir up once. Cover, cook at moderate simmer, without stirring, for 15-18 minutes, until the rice is tender and the liquid has evaporated. Discard bay leaf. Just before serving, add cream, simmer 1 minute, add cheese, fluff with fork.

VEGETABLE CASSEROLE

Peel one small potato and cut in ½ inch pieces. Same with 1 small yam, 1 small red bell pepper, 1 carrot. Toss lightly with olive oil, salt and pepper in 13 x 9 baking dish. Spread evenly. Top with thin slices of red onion; then thin slices zucchini (or not), drizzle with a little more oil, more salt and pepper. Arrange sliced tomatoes over top. Top with a Parmesan/bread crumb blend, drizzle again lightly with oil. Bake uncovered at 400° until tender and topping is golden brown, about 40 minutes. This can be served hot or at room temperature.

DR. MARTINI'S BRUSSELS SPROUTS

Ralph Higgins is a writer, columnist, and book/movie reviewer living in the Annapolis Valley of Nova Scotia. An avid cook as well as a voracious reader, he can often be found in his kitchen with a book in one hand and a wooden spoon in the other. Ralph writes:

"Among the local gay cognoscenti, Jim McMillan—nicknamed Dr. Martini, by me, for the lethal goodness of his cocktails—is known as a brilliant cook. An invitation to dine at the McMillan/Parker household is a guaranteed evening of delicious food and delightful company. This recipe for Brussels Sprouts is a favorite even among those who, as children, curled up their noses at these delightful little cabbages.

"Preparation is simple and takes very little time so I generally make it the last item to go on the table."

Preheat oven to 400°.

Wash and remove the stems and any discolored outer leaves from the Brussels Sprouts. Slice them—roughly into thirds. (Dr. M, who is a scientist, could probably tell you the thickness in centimeters. I tend to be rather more freestyle in my approach to slicing.)

In a cast iron skillet (a cast iron frying pan is an essential tool in the kitchen, in my opinion, but any frying pan which can go directly into the oven will work.) melt a large dollop of unsalted butter. (Must be unsalted as salted butter will burn more easily.) Put the Brussels Sprouts into the frying pan and stir slightly. Do not turn the slices over. You want them to brown and get a bit crispy without burning. Season with a dash of salt and pepper.

When the sprouts are just starting to brown, take them off the heat. Squeeze the juice of half a lime over them and place the pan in the oven to finish cooking. Remove after 3-4 minutes and serve immediately.

BRIAN CARDIN'S BAKED BEAN CASSEROLE

Another recipe from Nowell Briscoe, by way of a close friend.

2 (55-ounce) cans of Bush's Original Baked Beans
1 (16-ounce) package of bacon
1 big Sweet Vidalia Onion
4 tablespoons Dark Brown Sugar
Hearty Portion of Green Tabasco Sauce
½ of an (18-ounce) bottle of Bull's Eye Original BBQ Sauce

Freeze bacon overnight. Cut into small pieces after it is frozen. Fry bacon with minced onion and brown. Drain beans and pour into casserole dish. Add bacon/onion mixture. DO NOT STRAIN THE BACON GREASE! Add the remaining ingredients, making sure to break up any clumps of brown sugar and stir until dissolved. Sprinkle additional brown sugar on top of the dish and bake for 20 minutes at 325°. Cool down to a warm temperature and serve with burgers, pot roast, hot dogs, steaks for a delicious side dish.

THE GREEN BEAN CASSEROLE

Okay, I know this gets a lot of laughs, but many people wouldn't think of a holiday dinner without it, and, hey, I like it. I also have noticed that many of those people are laughing with their mouths full. For a change, try making it with a package of frozen broccoli florets instead of the green beans. The same foodies who sneered at the green beans will probably scarf it up. Those food queens can be awfully silly, you know.

16-20 ounces frozen green beans, defrosted and drained
1 can cream of mushroom soup
½ cup milk
1 teaspoon soy sauce.
Dash pepper
1 (2.8 ounces) can French fried onions

Combine soup, milk, soy sauce, and pepper in 1½ quart casserole dish. Add green beans and half the onions, toss to mix. Bake at 350 for 25 minutes, or until heated. Top with remaining onions, bake 5 minutes more.

▶ *Breads*

GRANDMA IMOGENE'S NUT BREAD

Ruth Sims, author of the Phoenix, *sends these poignant memories of her grandmother, along with Grandmother's recipe for nut bread:*

"*Her name was Imogene. She was born in 1883 and died in 1956, when I was in high school. She was 4'10" tall, with a Kewpie-doll look—dimples in her face, her hands, her elbows. She had a miserable marriage to a preacher who was mean to their second child (my mother) and was also a racist. In addition to leaving a well-off family to marry him and travel constantly from one small town to another, she had to deal with the devastating accident of her oldest child, who fell from a swing and shattered her legs. Though Imogene fought against it, the little girl's legs had to be amputated. She put boy's clothes on her crippled daughter so the little girl could hitch herself around (they didn't have money for a wheel chair for several years). As a result she faced criticism by church women for dressing a girl like a boy. Imogene had four children in eight years; the youngest one weighed 16 pounds when he was born.*

"*She was a gutsy little person. My favorite story of her is the time she silenced the sewing circle. The ladies had been sewing and gossiping as usual when Imogene abruptly got up and put her sewing work in her big workbasket. One of the ladies, shocked, asked, 'Sister, where are you going? The afternoon's still young.' To which my grandmother retorted, 'You've talked about everybody who's not here. I'm leaving so you can talk about me for a while.' And then there was the church lady who called upon the new preacher's wife. Imogene offered her a cup of coffee. The lady drew herself up and declared, 'I don't drink coffee. I'm a Christian!' Grandma's answer: 'So am I. But if there's coffee in hell and none in heaven, then I don't reckon I'll see you in the hereafter'.*"

2 cups sifted all purpose, unbleached flour
2 cups pastry or pastry blend flour (alternate: use 4 cups all purpose
    flour)
½ level teaspoon sea salt (alternate: ½ heaping teaspoon kosher salt)
1 teaspoon baking soda
2 teaspoons baking powder, aluminum free
2 cups light brown sugar, packed
2 cups low fat buttermilk
2 whole eggs, lightly beaten (or egg substitute to equal 2 eggs)
1 tablespoon vanilla (alternate: 1 tablespoon rum)
8 tablespoons unsalted butter, very soft (alternate: ½ cup Canola or
    Enova oil
1 cup Black or English walnuts, chopped

Preheat oven to 350°. Lightly grease two 8-inch loaf pans, or three 6-inch pans. Mix the flour, salt, baking soda and baking powder together and set aside. Combine the brown sugar, buttermilk, eggs, rum or vanilla, and butter or oil. If using an electric mixer, mix on low just to blend; if hand mixing, mix just enough to thoroughly blend. Either way, do not overmix, it will make the bread tough.

A half-cup at a time, add the flour mixture to the buttermilk mixture. Mix on low or stir until blended. Add walnuts, mix on low or stir until blended.

Pour into prepared pans, bake 40-50 minutes or until a tester comes out clean. Cool in pan on rack for 15 minutes. Then turn the bread out onto the rack for cooling. It will be almost mahogany brown and to-die-for.

I find it stores better for about 3 days wrapped in parchment paper and kept at room temperature. If you like it can be put in a plastic bag, but if wrapped in plastic without the parchment paper, the top gets sticky. It doesn't hurt anything, but if that happens, just leave it unwrapped for a few hours or even overnight. It's even better just a tad stale, believe it or not. It can be eaten at room temperature or heated up. I don't know how long it will keep because my family doesn't leave it around long enough to find out.

ORANGE BRAN FLAX MUFFINS

These are wonderfully healthy for you as well as being scrumptious. This makes a lot, and one or two of them is plenty to eat at one time (all that fiber!) but they can be frozen, too. You can get oat bran (not the same as oatmeal) and ground flaxseed at a health food store. Most supermarkets have wheat germ.

1½ cup oat bran
1 cup all purpose flour
1 cup ground flaxseed
1 cup wheat germ
1 tablespoon baking powder
½ teaspoon salt
2 oranges, cut into smallish pieces and seeded
1 cup brown sugar
1 cup buttermilk
½ cup oil (preferably grapeseed oil)
2 eggs
1 teaspoon baking soda
1½ cups golden raisins

Preheat over to 375°. Line 2 12-cup muffin pans with paper liners. In large bowl, combine oat bran, flour, flaxseed, wheat bran, baking powder and salt; set aside. In a blender or food processor, combine oranges, brown sugar, buttermilk, oil, eggs and baking soda, blend well (I have to do this in 2 batches in my blender); pour orange mixture into dry ingredients, mix until well blended (it will be gloppy). Stir in raisins. Divide among muffin cups; bake 18-20 minutes until a toothpick comes out clean. Cool in pans 5 minutes, before removing to a rack.

SMOKE HOUSE GARLIC BREAD

The Smoke House in Burbank, California, is justly famous for jazz in the lounge, great steaks, Prime Rib, and of course, garlic bread.

¼ pound butter
2 cloves garlic, minced or through a garlic press
Thickly sliced fresh bread, like French or Italian
Shredded American cheese

Melt the butter, add the garlic and let this stand for several hours or overnight. Drain off the garlic, and dip the bread in the butter, then into the cheese. Broil until heated and golden brown.

ONION FRENCH LOAVES

A good alternative for those who don't like garlic toast.

Split 2 loaves sourdough bread in half lengthwise. Cream 2 sticks butter and 1 package dry onion soup mix. Spread on cut sides of bread, wrap in foil (can be done ahead.) bake in 350 oven for 15 minutes. Open foil, bake 5 minutes more

BANANA BREAD

5 tablespoons butter
½ cup sugar
½ cup firmly packed brown sugar
1 large egg
2 egg whites
1 teaspoon vanilla
1½ cups mashed, very ripe bananas
1¾ cup flour
1 teaspoon baking soda
½ teaspoon salt
¼ teaspoon baking powder
½ cup heavy cream
⅓ cup chopped walnuts

Heat oven to 350°. Spray bottom only of 5 x 5 loaf pan. Beat butter in large bowl with electric mixer on medium, until light and fluffy. Add sugars and beat well. Add egg, egg whites, and vanilla. Beat until well blended. Add banana, beat on high 30 seconds. Combine flour, baking soda, salt and baking powder. Add to butter mix alternately with cream, ending with flour mixture. Add walnuts, mix well. Pour into prepared pan. Bake until brown and toothpick comes out clean, about 1 hour and 15 minutes. Cool on wire rack 10 minutes. Remove from pan, cool completely on wire rack

MAYO BISCUITS

Think it's too much trouble to whip up a batch of biscuits for your honey? Think again. Serve these hot out of the oven with lots of butter to slather on them. The easiest way to measure the milk and the mayonnaise, by the way, is to fill a measuring cup to the 1 cup line

with milk, and spoon mayonnaise into it, mixing, until the milk reaches the 1¼ cup line.

2 cups self-rising flour (or see my introductory notes)
1 cup milk
¼ cup mayonnaise

Mix all until just blended. Drop by spoonfuls in a small baking pan coated with nonstick spray, with biscuits touching. You should have 12-14 biscuits. Bake at 400 until browned, about 20 minutes.

HOECAKES

These got their name, I am told, because they were originally cooked on the blade of a hoe, held over the fire. I think this method is simpler but the next time you have an open fire and a hoe handy, be my guest. It is sure to get you noticed.

1 cup self-rising flour (or see my introductory notes—but, by this time, maybe you should think about buying a small bag of self rising floor)
1 cup self-rising cornmeal (or use Aunt Jemima's cornbread mix)
2 eggs
1 tablespoon sugar
¾ cup buttermilk
⅓ cup plus 1 tablespoon water
¼ cup vegetable oil or melted bacon grease (did I say they were healthy?)
Oil, butter, or margarine for frying

Mix all ingredients well except the frying oil. Heat the frying oil in a medium or large skillet over medium heat. Drop batter by full table-spoons into skillet, about 2 tablespoons batter per hoecake (or use a ¼ cup measuring cup, filled about half full for each one). Fry till brown and crisp; turn with spatula and brown other side. Remove with slotted spoon and drain on paper towel lined plate. Leftover batter will keep in fridge for up to 2 days.

POPOVERS

Though it is not absolutely necessary, you will get best results by making the batter at least an hour ahead and refrigerating. Re-blend or stir before pouring.

5 tablespoon unsalted butter, melted
3 large eggs
1 cup milk
1 cup flour
½ teaspoon salt

Put eggs in blender and blend at high speed 1 minute, until frothy. Add milk and remaining butter. Reduce speed and blend in flour and salt. Let rest (see above).

Preheat oven to 375°. Use 2 tablespoons butter to grease 12 muffin cups (2½ inch wide by 1¼ inches deep). Place muffin pans in oven for 2-3 minutes to preheat. Pour batter evenly into muffin pans, bake 25 minutes, or until browned. Make a small slit with the tip of your knife in the top of each to let out steam, and bake 10 minutes more. Remove from cups immediately. Serve hot with butter.

Popover tips: beat batter just until smooth, don't over beat; if muffin tins have less than 1 inch between cups, pour into every other cup. Fill cups ¾ to almost full, so batter can pop up over edges. Don't open the oven door to peek. Always puncture when they have puffed and shell has set and return to oven to firm up. Split larges ones open and spoon in scrambled eggs or, for dessert, split popover tops open and fill with ice cream, or fill with pastry cream and drizzle chocolate sauce on top.

LOW FAT POPOVERS

If you're watching your figure, these are a good substitute and they're still luscious. They can be frozen and reheated.

1 cup flour
½ teaspoon salt
1 cup milk
2 large eggs
1 tablespoon butter, melted
Cooking spray
1 teaspoon vegetable oil

Measure flour by spooning into a dry measuring cup, and level with knife. Combine flour and salt, stir with a whisk. Combine milk and eggs in bowl, stir with whisk till blended, let stand 30 minutes. Add to flour mix, stir well with whisk, stir in butter. Heat oven to 375°. Spray muffin tins with non-stick spray, brush evenly with oil. Place cups in oven for 5 minutes to preheat. Divide batter among prepared cups, bake at 375° for 30 minutes until golden, cut slits in tops and bake for 10 minutes more. Serve immediately.

CINNAMON COFFEE CAKE

This is the sort of thing that's ideal to fix on a cold, blustery day when you are alone in the house. That way you can eat the whole bloody thing and clean up the dishes and no one will be the wiser. Lock the bathroom scales in the attic and tell hubby they got stolen. Honesty has ruined many a good marriage. While you are at it, rub some Pine Sol behind your ears just before he gets home. It will mask the baking aromas and make you smell like you have been cleaning house all day. In place of his share of the coffee cake, give him something else he particularly enjoys. Well, how am I supposed to know what that might be? He's your hubby.

Filling and Cake:
⅓ cup packed light brown sugar
2 teaspoons ground cinnamon
½ cup chopped pecans or walnuts
1 package (18.5 ounces) plain yellow cake mix—*not* the one with pudding included.
1 package (3.4 oz) vanilla instant pudding mix
¾ cup vegetable oil
¾ cup water
4 large eggs
1 teaspoon pure vanilla
Bundt pan
Vegetable oil spray for misting the pan
Flour for dusting the pan

Glaze:
1 cup sifted confectioners' sugar
2 tablespoons milk
½ teaspoon vanilla

Place rack in center of oven and preheat oven to 350°. Lightly mist Bundt Pan with vegetable oil spray, dust with flour, shake out excess flour. Sprinkle the nuts in bottom of pan and set aside.

For the filling, place brown sugar and cinnamon in small bowl and stir to combine well. Set aside.

Place cake mix and pudding mix in a large bowl and stir together. Put oil, water, eggs and vanilla in another bowl, stir to combine, and add to cake mix. Beat with electric mixer on low speed 1 minute. Stop and scrape down sides of bowl. Beat for 2 minutes at medium speed, pausing to scrape sides down again if necessary. Pour ⅓ of batter into prepared pan. Scatter half of the filling evenly over the batter. Pour another ⅓ of batter evenly over filling. Scatter remaining filling on top. Pour the rest of the batter over the top. Bang pan on counter to level surface.

Bake until golden brown and springs back when pressed lightly with your finger, 50-60 minutes. Remove from oven and cool on wire rack 20 minutes. Run a knife around edges to loosen, invert on rack and remove from pan. Allow to cool completely, 30 minutes at least.

To prepare the glaze: Combine confectioners' sugar, milk and vanilla, stir to mix well. Place cake on serving platter and drizzle with glaze. Will keep covered 1 week at room temperature (Oh, right!)

SPOON BREAD

Is this simple or what? Nothing to chop or slice or even to measure—goes well with ham or pork chops or chicken. Heck, put it on your Easter bonnet. You'll be a standout at the parade.

1 cup (2 sticks) melted butter, cooled to room temperature
2 large eggs beaten slightly
1 (14¾ ounce) can of cream style corn
1 (15¼ ounce) can of whole kernel corn, drained.
1 (8 ounces) carton sour cream
1 (8½ ounce) package corn muffin mix

Preheat oven to 350°. Combine all ingredients and mix thoroughly. Pour into a 9 x 11 x 2 casserole, bake about 40 minutes or until lightly browned. Serves 10-12. For a variation, use Mexican style whole corn kernels.

MY GRANDMOTHER'S POTICA
(Pronounced "poh-tée-tsa")

This delightful sweet bread from old Slovenija was contributed by one of my editors (and fellow writers), Rob Reginald, who writes:
"*When I was a teen in Spokane, Washington, we would often visit my grandmother, Anna Kapel, who lived on Wabash Street in the Northern part of town. She would fix us all kinds of Mediterranean-style dishes that she'd learned to cook as a girl in the 'Old Country.' Potica was ever my favorite. Grandma could make it in a seemingly infinite variety of ways, depending on the contents of her larder. 'Apple potica' was a pastry version—and when apples weren't available, she'd sometimes use cottage cheese. But the bread style of potica was the one I really liked, and it was only recipe that she ever wrote down, alas.*"

1 cup water
1 cup canned milk
8 cups flour
2 eggs
½ cup butter, cut up
½ cup plus 1 teaspoon sugar
2¼ ounces yeast
½ cup warm water
2 teaspoons salt
5 cups walnuts, chopped
1½ pounds dates, pitted and chopped
2½ cups raisins
1¼ cups brown sugar, packed
½ cup butter, cut up
2 teaspoons vanilla
2 teaspoons cinnamon
2-3 eggs

Warm the milk and water in a saucepan. Beat 2 eggs with an egg-beater, and set aside. Put ½ cup butter and ½ cup sugar in large bowl. Add 2 teaspoons salt. When the milk has a skin, pour it into the bowl and stir to dissolve. Wait until it has cooled before proceeding. Mix the yeast packets into ½ cup warm water, add 1 tsp sugar, and stir lightly until frothy. Add to a large bowl, stirring to blend with other ingredients. Add 3 cups flour, using a sifter and stirring well. Add the beaten eggs and stir well. Add 3 more cups flour, stirring until dough is workable, and then turn out onto a floured board and knead. Kneading can take a while; continue adding flour to keep the dough from getting sticky. The dough will get shiny when about done. Oil another large bowl, and put in the dough, letting it rise until about doubled, usually an hour or so. You can also put it in a cold oven with a towel over the bowl and a pan of hot water below to assist the rising.

Meanwhile, put ½ cup butter into a saucepan. Add the brown sugar, and warm on medium low heat, stirring continuously while adding the dates and raisins. Continue stirring until the dates begin to cook down and become paste-like. When the mixture gets thick, add a little water to keep it pasty. Add the cinnamon and vanilla while cooking. When the raisin mix is pasty, stir it into the nuts. Add two beaten eggs to make it spreadable (you may need to add a third beaten egg).

Put the bread dough on floured board, punch it down, turn it over, and let it rise for 15 minutes. Divide the dough into 4 pieces with a sharp knife. Wrap 3 pieces in cloth and roll out 1 piece to 16 x 12 inches. Divide the filling in a bowl with a knife into 4 sections. Place dollops of ¼ of the filling on the rolled-out dough. Spread the filling evenly to the edges of the dough. Roll up the dough from the narrow end. Pinch the ends of the dough to seal, and place it seam side down in a greased 9 x 13 inch pan. Repeat with the other portions of dough and filling, placing 2 loaves side-by-side in each pan. Cover the pans with cloth, and put in a cold oven. Set a pan of hot water below bread, and allow it to rise until about double again for about 1 hour. Remove the pans. Heat an oven to 350°. Remove cloths from the pans, and bake the loaves for 35-40 minutes, or until golden brown. Remove from the oven, drizzle with melted butter or margarine, and serve.

Makes 4 loaves. Preparation time: 5 hours.

Robert Reginald has penned seven novels, including The Phantom's Phantom (Wildside Press, 2007), *the Nova Europa historical fantasies, and* Invasion!, *a story collection (*Katydid & Other Critters*), and numerous nonfiction works.*

▶ *Desserts*

PIE CRUSTS

Here is the simplest recipe ever for pie crusts—stop at the refrigerated section in your supermarket and buy a box of Pillsbury prepared crusts. They are very good and I doubt that any of your guests will know you didn't make them. I have included below some specialty crusts, and in the section of diabetic-friendly desserts, low carb versions of specialty crusts; but otherwise, I think you will find the Pillsbury crusts will do perfectly well for your baking needs.

GRAHAM CRACKER CRUST

Again, you can buy a prepared crust at your market, including a reduced fat version—but this is undoubtedly better, and not a lot of work.

1½ cups graham cracker crumbs (about 20 crackers)
3 tablespoons sugar
⅓ cup butter, melted

Preheat oven to 350°. Mix all together and press into 9-inch pie plate. Bake 10 minutes. Cool.

COOKIE CRUST

See notes, above.

1½ cups crushed cookies (vanilla, or chocolate wafers or gingersnaps)
¼ cup butter, melted

Preheat oven to 350°, mix all together and press into 9-inch pie place. Bake 10 minutes. Cool.

GRAPE TART

This is for when you really want to knock their socks off. It reads more complicated than it actually is. If you find the puff pastry part of it intimidating (but it really isn't that hard; you can always do a dress rehearsal the week before), use a regular pie shell, in which case, reduce initial cooking temperature to 415°; otherwise, the plan of attack is much the same. Since you can make the shells one day and freeze them, it is not much more trouble to make several at the same time, and the next time you want to do a tart, you will have the shell already at hand. There is a slightly different version of a puff pastry shell with the recipe for Asparagus Tart in the brunch section. That one is simpler and avoids the problem of the "walls" collapsing as the shell bakes; however, it makes a shallower shell. If you want something deeper, this is your choice. Puff pastry shells are a wonderful thing to have on hand, for both savory and sweet dishes. In place of grapes, for instance, you could put a layer of pastry cream in one of these deeper shells and top it with peach or pear halves that have been poached just enough to make them tender, and then glaze as here.

1 puff pastry shell (see above)
3 cups seedless grapes, white or red or (preferably) mixed, washed
    and stemmed
¾ cup sweet white wine such as Sauterne or Malvasia Bianca
3 tablespoons brandy or kirsch (optional)
1 (12-ounce) jar red currant jelly

Toss grapes with the wine and the brandy and macerate 2 hours. (If you are in a hurry, skip that part; this will still be lovely.) Drain thoroughly. Make the shell (see below). Heat the currant jelly and lightly brush the bottom and inner sides of the shell. Arrange the grapes in the shell, and glaze the top with more of the jelly.

PUFF PASTRY SHELL—ANOTHER WAY

1 sheet of Pepperidge Farm (or other) puff pastry

Follow the directions for thawing pastry. Cut strips ¾ inches wide from each side of the sheet. Paint a ¾ inch strip all around the edge of the remaining sheet with ice water and cut the strips to fit on the moistened edges, pressing down with the tines of a fork or the back of a knife, to attach to the bottom, and moistening the ends of the strips where they meet and pressing together lightly to attach. Cover and chill 1 hour. Prick the bottom of the shell at ¼ inch intervals with the tines of a fork. If it's taking you a while to prepare the fillings, pop the shell back in the fridge to keep it cool. You can also wrap the shell now carefully in Saran wrap and freeze, and bake later. If you bake it later, let it thaw to room temperature for 30 minutes before proceeding. Once baked, puff pastry is better eaten the same day.

To bake, preheat oven to 450°. Put the (thawed) shell on a baking sheet. Line the shell with nonstick foil, non-stick side down, and fill with pie weights or dried beans, being careful to cover the bottom but not to push the sides out. Bake about 20 minutes, until sides have risen and began to brown. If you cut your side strips ¾ inches wide and fastened them well, you shouldn't have any collapsing sides, but keep an eye on them. If you notice the sides tilting inward, prop them up with toothpicks; if outward, with some wadded up foil.

Remove from the oven, reduce heat to 400°. Remove (carefully) the foil and beans and prick the bottom again lightly. Bake 5 minutes longer, or until lightly browned and bottom is set. Remove from oven, let cool on the pan 10 minutes, and carefully slide onto a rack. Fill as above.

STRAWBERRY TART WITH ORANGE CREAM

1 baked 9-inch pie shell
8 ounces cream cheese (regular or low fat but not fat free) at room temperature
¼ cup sugar
1 teaspoon grated orange zest
2 teaspoons Cointreau (an orange liqueur; you can substitute Triple Sec, but it's not as good)
2 cups fresh strawberries, hulled and halved lengthwise
½ cup apricot jam

With an electric mixer, cream cheese and sugar until smooth. Mix in zest and Cointreau, spread over bottom of pie shell. Arrange strawberries on top. Heat jam in saucepan until it liquefies, pour through a mesh sieve to strain out fruit chunks (or you can leave the chunks in, they don't bother me), brush berries gently with a thin coating of jam. Refrigerate until ready to serve. Remove from fridge 20 minutes before serving.

EASY CHERRY TURNOVERS

These are awfully good and not very complicated to make. You will have left over cherry pie filling, which you can spoon on ice cream for an impromptu sundae. Oh, did you ever wonder how "sundae" got its name and that odd spelling. The ice cream soda became so popular in eighteenth-century America, religious leaders starting grumbling about people indulging in them on Sundays (spoil sports); so ice cream parlors began to make them without the soda, just the ice cream and the syrup in a dish, and to avoid offending the preacher, changed the spelling. Okay, I don't really know, it's just what I read, but it makes a good Sundae afternoon story, doesn't it?

1 package Pillsbury refrigerated piecrusts (2 crusts) at room temperature
1 package (3 ounces) cream cheese, softened
¼ cup confectioner's sugar
1 cup canned cherry pie filling
¼ teaspoon almond extract
Sugar

Preheat oven to 425°. Place piecrusts, one at a time, on lightly floured surface; use a wide mouthed jar to cut into circles at least 3½ inches in diameter, more if you've got a wider jar or container. Or use a saucer to trace an outline and cut the circles out with the tip of a paring knife. You will get about half a dozen circles out of the two crusts, although you can roll out the scraps again to make another one or two if you like. In a small mixing bowl, beat cream cheese and sugar until smooth. Spread about ½ teaspoon on one half of each pastry circle. Combine pie filling and almond extract. Place about 1 teaspoon atop the cream cheese on each circle (about 1 cherry and a bit of the juice.) Fold circles in half and crimp the edges with the tines of a fork to seal. Place on a baking sheet lined with non-stick foil or parchment paper. With the tip of a paring knife, cut 1-2 small slits in the top of each turnover and sprinkle each with a pinch of sugar. Bake for 12-14 minutes or until lightly browned. Remove to wire racks to cool. Refrigerate until serving time.

EASY AS APPLE PIE

This is simpler to make than the usual apple pie, and has the bonus of cutting the carbs and calories in half. You can adjust the sugar as you like, but I like to taste the fruit and not just sugar. I use a pizza stone in my oven whenever I bake pie, which helps cook the bottom crust faster so it doesn't get soggy. If you are using a traditional pie dish (this doesn't) you can set it directly on the preheated stone; in this case, you can set the baking sheet on the stone. It takes a while, at least half an hour, and a full hour is better, to heat up the pizza stone.

1 refrigerator pie crust
2 tablespoons sugar
2 tablespoons Splenda (or use all sugar)
2 tablespoons cornstarch
1-teaspoon ground cinnamon
4 cups peeled, thinly sliced apples (about 4 apples)
1 egg white, lightly beaten until frothy
1 teaspoon additional sugar
1 tablespoon butter, chilled and diced

Preheat the oven to 425°. Line a baking sheet with parchment paper or non-stick foil. Unroll the pie crust on the prepared baking sheet. Mix the sugar and Splenda, cornstarch and cinnamon in a small bowl. Toss with the apples to coat thoroughly. Heap the apples in the middle of the crust, leaving a 2-inch border all around. Fold the piecrust border roughly up over the edges of the apples. Brush the exposed top of the crust with the egg white and sprinkle with the extra teaspoon of sugar. Scatter the diced butter over the top of the apples. Bake for 20 minutes in the lower one third of the oven, or until the apples are tender when pierced with the tip of a paring knife and the crust is nicely browned. Cool for 5 to 10 minutes and transfer to rack or serving dish.

DO-IT-YOURSELF TIPSY PIE

1 Pillsbury piecrust, baked (or choose an appropriate specialty crust, see above)
1 cup sugar
1 envelope unflavored gelatin
4 eggs, separated

½ cup water
Flavorings (choose from the suggestions below)

In small saucepan stir ½ cup sugar and gelatin. Blend egg yolks with water and flavorings. Stir into sugar mixture, cook over medium heat, stirring constantly, until it comes to a boil. Remove from heat, cool and refrigerate until cool and thickened. Beat egg whites until foamy. Add remaining ½ cup sugar, 1 tablespoon at a time, beat until stiff and glossy. Fold gelatin mixture into egg whites and spoon into prebaked pie shell.

Flavorings:

Butterscotch Collins Pie: 5 tablespoons Scotch, 2 tablespoons Scotch liqueur, 1 tablespoon lemon juice, garnish with orange slices or maraschino cherries

Brandy Alexander Pie—5 tablespoons brandy, 3 tablespoons crème de cacao

Daiquiri Pie—5 tablespoons Golden rum, 2 tablespoons lime juice, 1 tablespoon lemon juice

Black Russian Pie—7 tablespoons Vodka, 3 tablespoons coffee liqueur

Coming through the Rye Pie—¼ cup rye or bourbon, ¼ cup orange juice, 2 tablespoons grated orange peel.

KEY LIME PIE

Line 9-inch pie plate with graham cracker crust, or buy a pre-made crust. Beat 6 egg yolks; add 1 cup lime juice (key lime juice if you can find it), 2 (14 ounces) cans sweetened condensed milk and 1 tablespoon grated lime rind. Pour into pie shell and freeze. Remove from freezer and spread with whipped cream. Let sit 5 minutes before serving.

RHUBARB CREAM CHEESE PIE

This could be done with almost any fruit: peaches, blackberries, etc.

4 cups rhubarb, cut in 1 inch pieces; or mix rhubarb and strawberries
3 tablespoons cornstarch
¼ teaspoon salt
1 cup sugar
9 inch unbaked piecrust

1 (8-ounce) package cream cheese, room temperature
2 eggs
½ cup sugar (in addition to the above)
1 cup sour cream
Toasted almonds for garnish (optional)

Preheat oven to 425°. In 2-quart saucepan, combine rhubarb, cornstarch, salt and 1 cup sugar; stirring often, cook until it boils and thickens. Pour into piecrust, bake 10 minutes. While piecrust is baking, combine cream cheese, eggs and ½ cup sugar and beat until smooth. Remove pie from oven and reduce temperature to 350°. Pour cream cheese mixture over rhubarb mixture. Bake at 350° for 30-35 minutes, until set. Cool on rack, and chill. To serve, spread sour cream on top and garnish with toasted almonds if desired.

CHESS PIE

This is another old-fashioned recipe that you don't hear of much anymore, I don't know why. It is traditionally American, and delicious.

9-inch piecrust, partially baked

For the filling:
1 cup plus 3 tablespoons sugar
1 tablespoon flour
1 tablespoon cornmeal
⅛ teaspoon salt
4 large eggs
5 tablespoons unsalted butter, melted
¼ cup half and half (or buttermilk, which gives it a nice tang)
½ teaspoon vanilla
2 tablespoons grated lemon zest
3 tablespoons lemon juice

In a large bowl stir sugar, flour, cornmeal and salt together. Add eggs, butter, half and half and vanilla; blend thoroughly, stir in lemon zest and juice. Pour into crust. Bake at 375° for about 40 minutes until custard is lightly brown on top and a knife comes out almost clean. Cool on rack. Serve at room temperature or chilled, with whipped cream if desired.

LEMON CUSTARD PIE

Couldn't be easier. You can also bake this without the crust, in individual custard cups or ramekins, which will reduce calories and carbs, and garnish those when serving with some fresh raspberries or blueberries Very pretty, and tasty.

3 large eggs
1¼ cups sugar
Lemon zest—grate one of the lemons below before you squeeze it
½ cup lemon juice (about 3-4 lemons)

Combine all the above in blender and blend just to mix, then add:
¼ cup melted butter—and blend again.
    Pour into an unbaked 8 or 9" pie shell, and bake at 350° for 30-35 minutes.

LEMONADE PIE

For the whipped topping, you can choose between regular, light, and sugar-free versions, as you like. The pie must be kept in the freezer, but set it out about 15 minutes before you are ready to serve it (depending on the room temperature) and keep an eye on it—it will melt if it gets too warm, and leave you with (still tasty) glop.

1 package whipped topping, thawed
1 (6-ounce) can frozen lemonade concentrate, thawed, undiluted
Yellow food color, optional
1 9-inch graham cracker crust

Stir the lemonade (and the food coloring, if using) gradually into the whipped topping, until thoroughly combined. Pour into the pie shell and freeze 4 hours or overnight (see notes, above.) For **Orange Pie**, use frozen orange juice concentrate and add ½ cup sugar, or to taste.

SWEET POTATO PIE

I like this better than the more customary pumpkin pie. You can leave out the rum, but it does seem a shame; I can't help thinking of those starving children in Haiti.

1 9-inch pie shell, unbaked
1 cup light brown sugar
3 large eggs
1 teaspoon cinnamon
½ teaspoon ground ginger
½ teaspoon freshly grated nutmeg
¼ teaspoon ground cloves
¼ teaspoon salt
1 cup sweet potato purée
1-2 tablespoons molasses
1-2 tablespoons rum, dark is better
¾ (about) cup heavy cream (see below)
Whipped cream for topping, if desired

To make sweet potato purée, peel 8-10 ounces orange fleshed sweet potatoes, then cut into 2-inch chunks. Steam for about 25 minutes or until tender. Rub through a wire sieve or put through a ricer. You can drain canned sweet potatoes (not the candied ones) and use them instead without much damage.

Position oven rack at lowest position, place pizza stone on rack and a 14 inch or so piece of foil (not heavy duty) on stone. Preheat at 400° for 30 minutes or longer. Combine brown sugar and eggs in a large bowl and whisk until smooth. Whisk in spices and salt, then the sweet potato purée. Put molasses (to taste) and rum (to taste) in bottom of measuring cup, fill to the 1 cup line with the heavy cream, stir to combine. Whisk thoroughly into sweet potato mixture. Pour into pie shell. Place on foil-lined pizza stone. Close oven door, reduce heat to 350°, and bake 40-50 minutes, until the sides are slightly risen and the center is fairly firm when jiggled. Halfway through cooking time, check and if crust rim is browning too quickly, bring foil up and loosely over crust (don't get carried away, you're not gift wrapping), leaving pie filling uncovered. When done, cool on a rack until completely cooled. May be stored covered and refrigerated for 2 days. Serve at room temperature with dollop of whipped cream, if desired, or with pumpkin ice cream.

MILLIONAIRE PIE

This dates from the Great Depression, and is so named because it is very rich, but especially because it was felt that only a millionaire could then afford the ingredients. Even today, it's a bit of an extravagance. Okay, it brings out the white trash in me.

1 (8-ounce) package cream cheese, softened
½ cup sugar, plus 3 tablespoons
Grated zest of 1 lemon
2 tablespoons lemon juice
1 cup chopped pecans, lightly toasted
1 cup sweetened flaked coconut
1 cup sliced strawberries, plus some whole ones for garnish
1 cup diced fresh pineapple or canned pineapple chunks, well drained and diced (do not used crushed)
1 cup heavy cream
½ teaspoon vanilla
1 9-inch graham cracker crust or just plain old Pillsbury's

Beat cream cheese, ½ cup sugar, zest, and lemon juice at high speed until smooth. Fold in pecans, coconut, strawberries and pineapple. Beat heavy cream, 3 tablespoons sugar, and vanilla in chilled bowl until stiff. Fold half the whipped cream into the cream cheese mixture. Pour into crust, top with rest of whipped cream, garnish with whole berries, refrigerate at least 4 hours.

QUICK BLACKBERRY COBBLER

You can do this with almost any frozen fruit.

Combine 2 bags frozen blackberries, thawed, with ½ cup flour. Add ½ cup butter cut in small pieces and 2 teaspoons vanilla. Pour into a baking dish. Cut refrigerated piecrust into strips ½ inch wide and place on top in a lattice-work pattern. Bake at 425° for 45 minutes.

EASY BOSTON CREAM PIE

Which isn't, of course, a pie at all, but a cake (don't ask me to explain, I have no idea) so I have put it here at the end of the pie section and the beginning of cakes, and you can think of it whichever way you like.

Make any 2 layer white or yellow cake, from scratch or a mix; freeze one layer for another time. Or, make this variation on Bisquick's classic Velvet Crumb Cake:

Grease and flour a 9 inch round or 8 inch square cake pan. Combine 1 ½ cups original Bisquick mix, ½ cup granulated sugar, ½ cup milk, 2 tablespoons shortening or butter, 1 teaspoon vanilla, and

1 egg in a large bowl and beat with an electric mixer for 30 seconds on low speed, to combine. Then beat on medium speed for 4 minutes, pausing occasionally to scrape the bowl. Bake 30-35 minutes, until a toothpick comes out clean. Cool, split horizontally, fill with vanilla pudding (make Jell-O instant if you like). Frost with this astonishingly easy Thin Chocolate Icing:

THIN CHOCOLATE ICING

Melt 1 square unsweetened chocolate (1 ounce) and 1 teaspoon butter over hot water; remove from heat, blend in 1 cup confectioners sugar and 2 tablespoon boiling water. Beat only until smooth but not stiff.

STEVEN HOFFMAN'S VICTORY PUMPKIN ROLL (WITH THANKS TO JMG)

Steven sends, along with this delicious recipe, the story of an office victory that ensued from it:

"Long Island, NY, 1994. I had never worked in an office where I was the only guy. Our office was 6 (women) to1 (me). New York women. Strong women. 'Hello, I'm in the room' became my mantra as my boss would comment on the run in her black stocking, or one of them would make similar woman-to-woman remarks. Mostly, I think they regarded me as some exotic species. Once or twice, I got the impression that they considered it a lesser species.

"One day my co-worker, Jeanie, brought in pumpkin rolls that she had made. Harmless pumpkin rolls. It was a hot August day and she wanted to test the recipe before Thanksgiving. Jeanie called us into the meeting room and presented her orange and white swirled masterpiece. I salivated instantly as the smell of pumpkin bread filled my nose.

"Jeanie sliced and handed out generously sized pieces of her pumpkin and cream cheese dessert. It was rolled like a giant Hostess Ho-Ho or a Neapolitan ice cream cake. Conjuring Miss Manners kept me from digging in until everyone was served. The first bite of my swirled cake and the hot August day was transformed into a cozy dining room, autumn colored décor, with a nearby fireplace crackling and the smell of nutmeg. Oh, that was tasty.

"Of course I jumped at the offer of a second piece. I told Jeanie how great her dessert was and, midst everyone's gushing, I added, 'Jeanie, maybe I can get your recipe so I can make this at home.'

"This got me some surprised looks and even a smirk or two, as if some of the women doubted that I, a mere man, could cook. 'I will give everyone the recipe,' Jeanie said. 'You can have it too, if you like.'

"The following Sunday, determined to prove that I wasn't some helpless Neanderthal in the kitchen, I picked up the required items from the store and began my culinary project. It didn't take a Ph.D. to follow the recipe. While the cake was baking and I was mixing the cream cheese filling, I smiled. It felt good to prove that a man could cook, too. The oven timer clanged and I removed my pumpkin cake from the oven. Thanksgiving sensations returned, as I smelled the roll even before seeing it. Setting the pan atop the stove, I stared in disbelief. Jeanie's cake had been light orange and spongy. Mine, just out of the oven, was pancake-thin and dark tan. I had followed the recipe to a 'T'—so, what did I do wrong?

"Because I had told everyone that I was going to bring in my pumpkin roll on Monday, I presented my dessert at the morning staff meeting as if everything was fine. But, when I unwrapped the treat and began to serve it to the ladies, they all laughed. I tried to take the moment in stride.

"'I don't know what happened,' I declared innocently. 'I followed the directions word for word. And it actually tastes good.' With forkfuls of cake, the ladies acknowledged that, while the cake did look weird, it actually tasted delicious. A minor-yet-still-humiliating victory, but I knew that they were all now fully convinced that cooking was a woman's business, and something a man should leave alone. I even had to wonder if maybe they weren't right.

"The next day Jeanie came into my office and handed me a recipe card. 'I forgot to include the baking powder in the recipe I gave everyone. That's why your cake didn't rise. I goofed.'

"By noon everyone had received a revised card. While I wasn't quite a hero, for the rest of the day I walked around the office a little taller, feeling redeemed. And after that, I shared many culinary treats with the ladies, and no one questioned whether a mere man might be able to cook.

"Oh—I've made the pumpkin roll many times since then, and it has always risen—and always been welcome wherever I take it, including the office."

For the cake:
3 eggs, beaten
1 cup sugar
⅔ cup canned pumpkin
1 teaspoon lemon
1 teaspoon baking powder
1 teaspoon ginger
½ teaspoon nutmeg
½ teaspoon salt
1 cup of chopped walnuts

Add the remaining ingredients except for the walnuts, to the beaten eggs, and fold all together. Spread in greased and floured jellyroll pan (10 x 15 x 1). Top with the chopped walnuts, and bake at 375° degrees for 15 minutes.

Sprinkle linen dish towel (not terrycloth) with powdered sugar. Place warm cake on towel upside down. Roll while still warm and then refrigerate.

For the Filling:
1 cup powdered sugar
6 ounces cream cheese
4 tablespoons butter, melted
½ teaspoon vanilla

Beat until smooth. Unroll cake when cool, and spread with filling. Re-roll and refrigerate. Can be frozen.

Steven A. Hoffman has lived in seventeen states and countries and has called South Dakota home since 1997. When not writing, Steve oversees a major regional cultural institution. He has curated performing arts series, festivals, events and presented individual performances for over 15 years. He has also worked and taught in Chicago, New York, Ann Arbor, and Madison. His writings have been in business and literary publications. Most recently, Steve's works were included in the anthologies, Charmed Lives: Gay Spirit in Storytelling *and* Literary Cash: Writings Inspired by the Legendary Johnny Cash. *Since living in SD his appreciation for country music, hunting, and fishing has grown steadily. In 2005, he and his partner Jason were married in Winnipeg, Canada, on a beautiful summer day in a park filled with life. Steve can be contacted at SH.writings@hotmail.com*

BASIC YELLOW CAKE

I know that purists sniff at using a cake mix. I don't, but I will grant that no cake mix has the "crumb" of a scratch cake and really, if you try this recipe, you will find that making a good cake from scratch is not much more trouble than the mix.

2½ cups all-purpose flour
¼ cup cornstarch
4 teaspoons baking powder
½ teaspoon salt
1 cup milk
3 large eggs
2 teaspoons vanilla
2 sticks butter (16 tablespoons) softened
2 cups sugar

Put rack in middle of oven, heat to 350°. Grease and flour 2 8-inch pans. Mix first 4 ingredients in large bowl. Mix milk, eggs and vanilla in measuring cup. With an electric mixer, beat softened butter into dry ingredients, *first on low*, then increase to medium until it forms pebble size pieces. Add about ⅓ of milk mix, beat on low until smooth. Add remaining milk mix in 2 stages, beat on medium until batter is just smooth. Add sugar, beat until just incorporated, about 30 seconds. Divide batter between 2 pans. Bake about 40-45 min, until toothpick comes out clean. Cool on wire rack 5 minutes. Unmold, cool completely, at least 1 hour. The layers can be double wrapped in Saran wrap and kept for one day at room temp, or frozen for a few weeks.
Now, that wasn't so difficult, was it?

AUNT LOIS'S CHOCOLATE CAKE

Another recipe from Ken Beemer, Norfolk's organ technician (I don't know why I like to say that—VJB) who says: "Sounds strange, I know—putting vinegar and coffee in a chocolate cake, but it's really good!"

3 cups all purpose flour
2 cups sugar
½ cup of cocoa powder
2 teaspoons baking soda

1 teaspoon salt
⅔ cup canola oil
2 tablespoons white vinegar
2 cups strong black coffee
3 teaspoons of vanilla

Combine first 5 ingredients (flour through salt) and mix well. Add remaining ingredients. Bake at 350° for 25-30 minutes.

ISABELL'S FRESH APPLE POUND CAKE

Nowell Briscoe sends this wonderful recipe, with a bit of history included:

"*This was my Grandmother's most favored dessert. She often served this during Thanksgiving and Christmas and if a special occasion were to come due, one of these cakes would come from her kitchen to represent her.*

"*Let me give you some background on my Grandmother Blanche (how I DO love that name): she was my father's mother and truly a woman of Southern gentility if there ever was one. There were two things she cared about greatly during her life: playing bridge and reading. Her sister, my great aunt, was the librarian in my hometown and was the one responsible for my learning to love and appreciate books. But Blanche's great passions were bridge and books. Never in the years prior to her death when I knew her as a small child did I ever one time see her actually in the kitchen of the large home with its wide, sweeping front porch and manicured grounds. The kitchen was left entirely in the care of her cook, the treasured and beloved Isabell, for whose culinary expertise my grandmother took ALL the credit. Isabell and her husband (who cared for the grounds of the house and acted as driver and all-around handyman for the place) lived in a three-room building at the very back of my grandparents' property and were there at their beck and call.*

"*Being a bridge-lover, it was nothing uncommon for my grandmother to have three, four or five tables of bridge going nearly every weekday afternoon. In the summer the wide front porch would host three or four tables of bridge with perhaps another table or two in the living room. With many if not most of the town's most prominent women at my grandmother's house on any given day, there was always food being prepared to offer these doyennes of card games, be it a tempting salad, a fruit course or dessert with ice cream. As the weather turned colder, Isabell kept that old stove in the kitchen hot as a firecracker as pies and cakes were pulled from that oven to serve the ladies of the town.*

"Isabell came to my grandmother after her mother, my great grandmother, died and she stayed with Blanche until she died in 1953. After my grandmother died she came to cook for my parents until old age took its toll and she died in the early 1960s. Two of my favorite photos of Isabell show her coming from the kitchen into the dining room either one Thanksgiving or Christmas with the turkey on the platter to be laid before my grandfather to carve. Another photo showed Isabell in a relaxed moment in the back yard, her apron on and her hair pulled into a tight bun. She was a true magician in the kitchen and the few recipes that have survived during her time with my family are treasured and beloved among remaining family members.

"Of all the food Isabell produced from my grandmother's kitchen, the most asked for and the cake of the highest regard had to be her fresh apple pound cake with Brown Sugar Topping. Even as a child I would have rather eaten the topping than the cake, it was that good. Once you make this recipe, you will understand why. It is one of the best cakes I have EVER eaten and my aunt, now in her 80s, still makes this at Thanksgiving as a tribute to Isabell."

1 teaspoon cinnamon
3 cups all purpose flour, spooned into a cup
1 teaspoon baking soda
1 teaspoon salt
1½ cups of corn oil
2 cups sugar
3 large eggs, room temperature
2 teaspoons vanilla
1¼ cups medium-fine chopped pecans
2 cups pared and finely chopped apples

Sift flour, soda, and salt onto a platter or waxed paper. In large bowl beat oil, sugar, eggs, and vanilla at medium speed (with electric mixer) for 3 or 4 minutes until well blended. Gradually add flour mixture and beat until smooth. Fold in pecans and apples. Pour batter into a greased and floured pan (bundt pan in today's world). Bake in a preheated oven at 325° for about one hour and 20 minutes, or until a toothpick comes out clean. Cool for twenty minutes. For parties or other occasions, dribble Brown Sugar Topping over warm cake. The Brown Sugar Topping is as good as the cake.

BROWN SUGAR TOPPING

½ cup butter or margarine
½ cup firmly packed light brown sugar
2 teaspoons milk

Combine all ingredients and bring to a boil over medium heat. Cook two minutes, stirring constantly. Spoon hot sugar mixture over warm cake. If not served immediately, the topping will form a hard glaze over the cake that might make the cake hard to slice, but is good nonetheless.

VICTOR'S BEST CARROT CAKE

You could cut back or cut out the coconut, walnuts or raisins, though I like this just as is; but don't change the pineapple. The cake is very rich, so you don't really have to frost it, but of course I do, with a cream cheese frosting. This is positively the best carrot cake you've ever tasted.

2 cups all purpose flour
2 teaspoons baking powder
1 teaspoon baking soda
½ teaspoon salt
1 teaspoon cinnamon
½ teaspoon ground nutmeg
½ teaspoon allspice
4 eggs
2 cups white sugar
2 teaspoons vanilla
1 ¼ cups vegetable oil
2 cups grated carrots
1 (20-ounce) can crushed pineapple, drained
½ cup sweetened, flaked coconut
1 cup chopped walnuts (optional—some can't eat them)
1 cup raisins

Preheat oven to 350°; coat a 13 x 9 x 2-inch baking pan with spray. In a medium bowl, stir flour, baking powder, baking soda, salt, cinnamon, nutmeg and allspice together and set aside. In a large bowl, by hand, mix eggs, sugar and vanilla; stir in the oil; it will resemble a pudding. Gradually stir in the dry ingredients, then fold in well the carrots, pineapple, coconut, walnuts and raisins. Pour into pan, spread evenly. Bake 55-60 minutes or until a toothpick comes out mostly clean. Use a cream cheese frosting, if you like. Cool before frosting.

CHOCOLATE ZUCCHINI CAKE

I know that many cooks scoff at cake mixes. These people probably have far more time than the rest of us. When I come home from a shift standing by that lamppost, I want something quick and tasty. This cake takes all of five minutes to assemble, and I've never served it to anyone who didn't love it.

Make a Devil's Food Cake from a Duncan Hine's package mix (or another brand), exactly as instructed on the box (either the cholesterol version, or no cholesterol, your choice). To your batter, add 1 cup of grated zucchini, and follow the directions on the box for baking. When cooled and removed from the pan (again following Mister Hine's instructions) you can sprinkle this with powdered sugar if you're in a hurry, or make the following very easy frosting.

EASY CHOCOLATE FROSTING

Chocolate chips are perfect, but you can use almost any chocolate except unsweetened. If you use block chocolate, break or chop it first into small chunks

10 ounces of chocolate
4 ounces unsalted butter

Put the chocolate in the top of a double boiler over barely simmering water, to melt. When just melted, whisk in the butter until creamy smooth and spreadable. If it seems too thin, add a little more chocolate, or a little more butter if it's too thick. You can make this ahead and refrigerate it or freeze it, and just heat it gently to use (I have heated it in the microwave at the lowest setting, one minute at a time, stirring after each moment, again just until it's spreadable.)

ANOTHER SUPER EASY CHOCOLATE FROSTING

1½ cups Nestlé's semisweet chocolate chips
1½ cups sour cream, at room temperature

Melt chocolate chips in a double boiler, then cool to room temperature. Stir in the sour cream, ¼ cup at a time, until smooth.

BLACK WALNUT CAKE

This is a dense, pound cake kind of cake, not terribly sweet; you could glaze it but I don't think it needs it—on the other hand, I quite like a slice toasted and slathered up with butter. It is also, by the by, a dense batter, so if your mixer doesn't have a strong motor you'll likely end up doing a lot of the mixing by hand. And it's better the second day when the walnuts have really permeated the cake. Black walnuts have a slightly bitter taste; you could make this with something else, but what is the point of making a black walnut cake with, say, pecans?

2 cups white sugar
½ pound (2 sticks) butter, softened
4 eggs, separated
2 teaspoons vanilla
3 cups all purpose flour
2 teaspoons baking powder
Pinch salt
1 cup milk
1-1½ cups black walnuts, chopped but not too small

Preheat oven to 400°. Grease and flour a large tube pan or bundt pan. In large bowl, thoroughly cream butter and sugar until you cannot feel granules when rubbed between your fingers and it is a very pale color—about 4 minutes. Add egg yolks and vanilla and mix well.

In another bowl, combine flour, baking powder and salt. Add flour mixture and milk alternately to sugar mixture, stirring each addition just until blended—the cake gets tough if over mixed. Beat egg whites until very foamy but not at all stiff; gently fold into batter. Add walnuts, folding just until they are fully incorporated but again not over mixing the batter. Pour into prepared pan and bake for 45-60 minutes (check after 45) until a toothpick in the center comes out clean. Cool on wire rack for 10 minutes. Remove from pan and cool completely on rack before slicing. Wrapped well this keeps up to five days in a cool dark place. (Right!)

BANANA CAKE

If you can find LorAnn banana crème flavor, use that in place of the imitation banana flavor in the frosting. LorAnn is an East Coast product, and hard to find in the West. If you can't find it, the super-market stuff is fine. You could make the cake without the banana li-queur, but it really is better with. (Besides, the banana liqueur is also good on ice cream, or bananas sautéed in butter and brown sugar.) If you omit it, add 1 teaspoon Banana flavoring to the batter instead.

Shortening and flour to grease the pan
1 (18¼-ounce) package plain yellow cake mix
½ cup packed light brown sugar
1 teaspoon Cinnamon
2 medium size ripe bananas, mashed (about 1 cup)
1 cup water
½ cup vegetable oil
3 large eggs, lightly beaten
2 teaspoons Crème de banane liqueur

Heat oven to 350°. Lightly grease and flour a 13 x 9-inch baking pan. In large bowl combine cake mix, brown sugar and cinnamon. Add mashed bananas, 1 cup water, oil, eggs, and liqueur. Blend with electric mixer for 1 minute at low speed. Scrape down sides of bowl and beat 2 minutes at medium speed, till well blended, scraping bowl again if necessary. Pour into pan and bake on center rack of oven about 40 minutes, till top is lightly browned and a toothpick comes out clean. Cool on wire rack. Frost with the following:

BANANA CREAM CHEESE FROSTING

4 ounces cream cheese, at room temperature
½ stick (4 tablespoons) butter at room temperature
1¾ cups confectioners' sugar
3-4 drops imitation banana flavoring (see note, above)
Optional: chopped walnuts or pecans

In large mixing bowl, blend cream cheese and butter on low speed until well combined. Add confectioners' sugar a little at a time and beat on low speed until well blended, about 1 minute. Add flavoring and beat on medium speed until fluffy, about 1 minute more. Use at once to frost top of cake. Sprinkle if desired with chopped nuts.

HARVEY WALLBANGER CAKE

At one time there were dozens of these cakes flavored like popular drinks. Some of them were downright vile, but this is a good one, and just about anybody can do it

Mix together:
1 3¾-ounce package Jell-O instant vanilla pudding mix
1 package Duncan Hines Orange Supreme Cake
Mix together:
¼ cup Galliano
¼ cup Vodka
½ cup oil
¾ cup Orange juice

Preheat oven to 350°. Combine the two mixtures. Add 4 eggs one at a time, beating after each addition. Grease and flour 10-inch tube pan, pour batter into pan, and bake 45-50 minutes. Glaze.

For the glaze, combine:
1 cup powdered sugar
1 tablespoon orange juice
1 tablespoon Galliano
1 tablespoon vodka, if needed to thin out

PINE NUT TORTA

This is super good and somewhat different, almost like a giant cookie, and not terribly sweet. You can serve it with the Marsala Poached Fruit (recipe follows) or almost any fresh fruit, but, really, it's terrific just as it is.

3 large egg yolks
1 large egg
1½ teaspoons (packed) grated lemon peel
1 teaspoon vanilla

¼ teaspoon salt
10 tablespoons unsalted butter, room temperature
1 cup sugar
1½ cups unbleached all purpose flour
¾ cup pine nuts (about 3-4 ounces, but it needn't be exact)
Powdered sugar

Position rack in center of oven, heat to 375. Butter and flour 10-inch spring-form pan. Whisk egg yolks, egg, lemon peel, vanilla, and salt in small bowl to blend. Using electric mixer, beat butter and 1 cup sugar until pale and creamy. Gradually add flour, beating until it resembles coarse meal. Using a spatula, gently stir egg mix into butter mix and spoon into prepared pan; smooth top. The batter will be very thick and the cake will be very thin; don't let either disconcert you. Sprinkle pine nuts on top, press down lightly into the batter. (Oh, for heaven's sake, Dorothy, use your fingers.) Bake about 30 minutes, until a toothpick comes out clean. Transfer to rack, run knife around edges, remove pan sides, cool completely. Sprinkle with powdered sugar. Serve with Marsala Poached Fruit if desired.

MARSALA POACHED FRUITS

3 cups water
1 cup sweet Marsala wine
¼ cup sugar
1 cinnamon stick
1 (4-inch) strip lemon peel
2 cups pitted prunes
2 cups dried apricots (Or use any dried fruit you like)

Combine water, Marsala, sugar, cinnamon, and lemon peel in heavy large saucepan, bring to boil, stirring until sugar dissolves; add prunes and apricots, reduce to medium heat, simmer until fruit is soft but not mushy, stir frequently, about 25 minutes. Transfer fruit to bowl, boil liquid until syrupy, about 5 minutes longer, and pour over fruit. Can be made 2 days ahead and chilled. Bring to room temperature before serving. This is also good with a plain pound cake or rice pudding.

MAYONNAISE CAKE

This is my mother's recipe and one of her favorites. At one time Mayonnaise Cake was quite popular. It is as easy as a mix, and has the crumb of a scratch cake. You can use any chocolate frosting, or make a confectioner's sugar frosting and beat peanut butter into it to taste. My niece, Becky Kisling, won the blue ribbon at the county fair with this recipe. She specifies Baker's cocoa, by the way, and see my introductory notes on vanilla.

Combine:
3 cups sifted flour
6 tablespoons cocoa
1½ cups sugar
3 teaspoons baking powder

Combine:
1½ cups mayonnaise
1½ cups lukewarm water
1½ tsp vanilla

Add liquid ingredients to dry and beat until smooth. Pour into 2 greased and floured 8- or 9-inch cake pans, or one loaf pan. Bake 35 minutes until a toothpick comes out clean.

SINGLE-SERVING CHOCOLATE RASPBERRY CAKE

So, you are between assignments, so to speak. You are sleeping alone. What's more, you are eating alone. Which means, you buy an entire chocolate raspberry cake from the bakery, and consume it all in a fit of self-pity—or, you could try this. It takes several steps, but those will have your mind occupied for a bit with something other than HIM—and you'll have something to satisfy the most demanding sweet tooth, and then it's gone, and nothing to call you out of bed in the middle of the night. Okay, it's not exactly the same as having him back, but, face it, sweetie, the likelihood is the chocolate raspberry cake will be with you longer. Just try getting it off your hips.

⅓ cup chilled heavy cream
½ teaspoon sugar
⅛ teaspoon vanilla
5 chocolate wafers, such as Nabisco Famous

⅓ cup fresh raspberries
For garnish, grated bittersweet chocolate

Beat cream with sugar and vanilla until it just holds stiff peaks. Spread 1 heaping teaspoon of the cream onto each of 4 wafers. Arrange enough raspberries side by side as close as possible on one of the cream topped wafers to form an even layer. Stack 2 cream topped wafers on a plate, cream sides up, and top with the berry-covered wafer, then carefully spread another teaspoon of cream over berries. Top with last cream topped wafer and cover the cream with remaining plain wafer. Frost top and sides of "cake" with remaining cream. Cover with an inverted bowl and chill at least 4 hours. Serve with remaining berries. Pretty, and tasty. And no messy divorce.

DEVILS FOOD COOKIES

These are among the best chocolate cookies ever, especially if you have one still warm, BUT, beware, the dough is especially thick and can tax a small hand mixer. If you have friends who can't tolerate nuts (I do) the cookies will suffer no great harm if you leave out the pecans, though they are certainly better for their inclusion.

1 box Devils food cake mix (18¼ ounces)
2 eggs
¼ cup hot coffee
½ cup oil
2 tablespoons flour
1 cup semisweet chocolate pieces
1 cup chopped pecans
¾ cup bits of chocolate toffee candy (such as Heath bars, but not the packaged Heath bits, which are the toffee only, without the chocolate)

Heat oven to 350°. Combine cake mix, eggs, coffee, oil, and flour in large bowl. Beat on low speed until moistened. Beat on high for 2 minutes. Dough will be sticky. Fold in chocolate pieces, pecans and candy. Using about half the batter, drop by heaping tablespoons onto an ungreased baking sheet, 2 inches apart. Bake 12-14 minutes. Let cool on baking sheet until firm. Transfer to wire rack, cool; repeat with remaining batter. These are at their best still slightly warm.

LIME MELTAWAYS

These are great, but the dough can be crumbly and difficult to slice; if that happens, just form cookie rounds with your hands, Princess.

¾ cup (1½ sticks) unsalted butter, room temperature
1 cup confectioners' sugar
2 tablespoons fresh squeezed lime juice, plus grated zest of 2 limes
    (hint: grate the limes first)
1 tablespoon vanilla
1¾ cups plus 2 tablespoons all-purpose flour
2 tablespoons cornstarch
¼ teaspoon salt

In the bowl of an electric mixer fitted with whisk attachment, cream butter and ⅓ cup sugar until fluffy. Add lime juice, zest, and vanilla; beat until fluffy.

In medium bowl, whisk together flour, cornstarch and salt. Add to butter mixture and beat on low speed until combined.

Between two 8 x 12 pieces of parchment paper, roll dough into two 1¼ inch diameter logs. Chill overnight.

Heat oven to 350°. Line two baking sheets with parchment paper. Place remaining sugar in resealable plastic bag. Remove parchment from logs; slice into ¼-inch thick rounds. Place rounds on sheets, spaced 1 inch apart.

Bake until barely golden, about 15 minutes. Transfer cookies to wire rack to cool slightly, 8-10 minutes. While still warm, place cookies in sugar-filled bag, toss *gently* to coat. Bake or freeze remaining dough. Store cookies in airtight container up to 2 weeks. Makes about 10 dozen.

CHERRY BISCOTTI

These are particularly festive for Christmas, but I see no reason why you couldn't use another kind of candied fruit at other times of the year. I like them better without the chocolate chips, but I will include them here and you can make up your own mind.

¾ cup sugar
½ cup butter, softened
2 teaspoons almond extract
3 eggs

3 cups all purpose flour
2 teaspoons baking powder
2 cups candied green or red cherries, or mixed, cut in half
½ cup miniature chocolate chips, optional

Heat oven to 350° and lightly grease a cookie sheet or cover with parchment. Beat butter and sugar in a large bowl with electric mixer on medium speed until well blended. Beat in almond extract and eggs. Stir in flour and baking powder. Stir in cherries and chips if using. Shape dough into two 10" rolls. Place the rolls 5 inches apart on cookie sheet and flatten each to 3 inches in width. Bake 20-25 minutes until set and light golden brown (it takes more like 30 in my oven, but it's slow; just peek at them); Cool 10 minutes, then cut into ½ inch slices diagonally with a serrated knife. Turn slices cut side down on cookie sheet and bake 8-10 minutes (takes about 12 in my slow oven) until bottoms begin to brown; turn onto the other cut side and bake about 5-10 minutes longer or until browned and crisp. Makes about 3 dozen heavenly and not-too-sweet cookies.

FIG COOKIES

I love these. They are the grown-up version of Fig Newtons. They can also be made with fresh figs, or with dried dates, prunes or apricots.

¾ cup butter
½-¾ cup sugar (use the smaller amount if filling is very sweet)
2 eggs
1 teaspoon vanilla
2½ cups sifted all-purpose flour
½ teaspoon salt
1 teaspoon baking powder
1 cup or more of filling

Cream the butter, then cream with the sugar until fluffy. Beat in the eggs and vanilla. Sift the flour again with the salt and baking powder and stir into butter/sugar mixture just until blended. Chill. Remove half the dough at a time from the refrigerator. Roll about ⅛ inch thick on floured pastry cloth or board. Cut into rounds with floured cutter; divide rounds into 2 equal batches. With a thimble or the tip of a paring knife, cut holes in the center of half the rounds. Spoon from ¼ to 1 teaspoon filling into the center of the solid rounds, cover each with a round with a hole in the center, and press edges together with a fork, to seal. Or cut the rounds 3-4 inches in diameter, place filling on one half and fold over, crimp the edges. Place filled cookies on greased baking sheet, bake at 375º for 8-12 minutes. Remove from pan while warm and cool on rack.

FIG, DATE, PRUNE, OR APRICOT FILLING

½ pound dried figs or other fruit
1¼ cups water
1 cup white or firmly packed brown sugar
1 tablespoon lemon juice
½ cup finely chopped walnuts, pecans, almonds, filberts, or brazils (optional)

Bring dried fruit and water to a boil in saucepan, cover and simmer about 10 minutes until soft. Mash while warm, or cool and chop. Return to pan, add sugar and simmer until thick. Remove from heat, stir in lemon and nuts if desired (they will have more flavor if toasted lightly. Cool the filling before filling cookies.

ORANGE LACE COOKIES

¼ cup light corn syrup
¼ cup packed light brown sugar
¼ cup unsalted butter
1 tablespoon Cointreau
½ cup plus 2 tablespoon all purpose flour
1 tablespoon orange zest, grated or finely chopped—about 1 orange
⅛ teaspoon salt

Preheat oven to 350º. Place parchment paper on baking sheet and set aside. Combine corn syrup, sugar, butter and Cointreau in a small saucepan. Stir over low heat until butter melts. Remove from heat and add flour, orange zest and salt, and stir to combine. Drop by teaspoons on baking sheet, about 2½ inches apart. Place in oven, bake about 14 minutes, until cookies spread out, bubble and turn golden brown. Watch carefully after 10 minutes. Remove from oven and let stand until cookies firm slightly, about 4 minutes. If they have run together, use paring knife to separate gently. Remove to wire rack and let cool completely, until crisp. Repeat until all batter is used, stirring batter between batches. Store in airtight container up to 2 days. Makes 2-3 dozen.

RALPH HIGGINS SUGAR PLUMS

Ralph sends these two delicious recipes, and says:
   "In the famous poem, visions of these were said to dance in the heads of children on Christmas Eve. My own fondness for sugar plums dates from seeing Baryshnikov in tights in a performance of The Nutcracker. *(Sugar Plums indeed!—VJB).*
   "Here are two recipes for Sugar Plums. Preparation is essentially the same for both and only the ingredients vary slightly. They require no baking but you will need a food processor. I like to make both kinds to serve at my Holiday Open House. They always disappear quickly. Storage time will enhance the flavors."

FIG AND COCOA SUGAR PLUMS

⅓ cup of slivered almonds (2 ounces)
4 ounces dried figs
2 tablespoons unsweetened cocoa
½ teaspoon ground cinnamon
¼ cup liquid honey
1 tablespoon grated orange peel (I add strips of orange peel into the
   food processor)
½ teaspoon almond extract
¼ cup granulated sugar

In a small dry skillet, over medium heat, toast the almonds to bring out their flavor. Watch carefully. This takes only 5 to 10 minutes. Remove from heat. Cool.
   When almonds are cool enough to handle, add them with figs, cocoa, orange peel and cinnamon to food processor. Pulse until about the size of peppercorns. Add the honey and almond extract. Pulse 3-4 times, until a sticky mixture has formed.
   Pinch dough into 1-inch balls and roll in sugar in a shallow dish.
   Make a week ahead of time and keep in a sealed dish in the refrigerator to let the flavors mature.

APRICOT AND DATE SUGAR PLUMS

The second recipe uses apricots and dates rather than figs, has a few more spices and omits the cocoa. Makes a slightly larger batch.

2 cups almonds (toast in frying pan as in previous recipe)
¼ cup of honey (more may be needed. Adjust to get a sticky mixture. If too dry the plums won't hold their shape.)
2 teaspoons grated orange zest or peel
1½ teaspoons ground cinnamon
½ teaspoon ground allspice
½ teaspoon grated nutmeg
1 cup dried apricots
1 cup pitted dates
1 cup confectioners sugar

Prepare as in previous recipe. Roll in confectioners' sugar. Refrigerate on waxed paper in the refrigerator.

Ralph Higgins is a writer, columnist, and book/movie reviewer living in the Annapolis Valley of Nova Scotia. An avid cook as well as a voracious reader, he can often be found in his kitchen with a book in one hand and a wooden spoon in the other.

DEATH BY CHOCOLATE

The ultimate junk food—rich, sweet, and calorie-and cholesterol-laden—in other words, scrumptious! And, look, it's all packaged or ready-made stuff. Is this my kind of recipe, or what? The ideal serving bowl, by the by, is a large glass one, so the layers can be seen and admired, but don't worry, if they like chocolate, after the first bite, they'll eat this from a trough.

1 (19.8-ounce) package Fudge Brownie Mix
3 (3.5-ounce) packages instant chocolate mousse mix (each makes four ½ cup servings)—I like Knorr
8 chocolate/toffee candy bars (Heath, for example, or Score)
1 (8-ounce) carton whipped cream topping, thawed.

Bake brownies per package directions and cool. Prepare Mousse per package directions. Break candy into pieces (I like to set a few pieces aside, crush them fairly fine, and sprinkle on top at the end). Break brownies into pieces. Put half in bottom of bowl. Top with half the mousse, half the candy, half the topping. Repeat. Sprinkle top with crushed candy. This is really best if it chills for an hour or two.

CLASSIC BROWNIES

Brownies are perennial favorites, because they taste good and are almost foolproof to make. As long as you keep the flour to a minimum and never add chemical leavening (like baking powder) you will be fine.

3 ounces unsweetened chocolate
8 tablespoons (1 stick) unsalted butter, more for greasing baking pan
1 cup sugar
2 eggs
½ cup flour
Pinch salt
½ teaspoon vanilla

Heat oven to 350°. Combine chocolate and butter in small saucepan over very low heat, stirring occasionally. When chocolate is just about melted, remove from heat and continue to stir until smooth. Meanwhile, grease 8-inch square pan. Line it with waxed paper or parchment paper if you like and grease that. Transfer chocolate to bowl, stir in sugar. Beat in eggs, one at a time. Add flour, salt and vanilla. Stir to incorporate. Stop stirring when no traces of flour can be seen. Pour into pan, bake 20-30 minutes or until set and barely firm in middle. Cool on rack before cutting. If you like nuts—no puns—stir them into the batter just before pouring into the baking pan. Because I have friends who can't eat nuts, I make the brownies without and then stick a half a walnut or pecan on the top of about half the brownies.

ICE CREAM COOKIES

Okay, these are for the kid in you. They are fun, too. You might offer them to your guests as a do-it-yourself dessert, with an assortment of ice creams and cookies. Not, I suggest, at the table with your best linen. Sometimes bringing the guests into the kitchen makes for a better party.

Shape softened ice cream (see suggestions below) into discs; dip edges in filling; and place between two cookies:
    Dip Strawberry ice cream in minced dried strawberries, sandwich between two snickerdoodle cookies

Dip vanilla ice cream in crushed chocolate chips and use chocolate chip cookies.

Dip chocolate ice cream in chopped salted peanuts, use peanut butter cookies.

VICTOR'S CHOCOLATE BREAD PUDDING

This is probably not for the beginner, but it is awfully nice. Makes 12 servings.

⅔ cup plus 1 tablespoon sugar
1 cup heavy cream
8 ounces semisweet chocolate, coarsely chopped
5 eggs, separated
1 stick (¼ pound) unsalted butter, cut into pieces
1 tablespoon vanilla
2 cups fresh bread crumbs, made from about 5 slices firm textured
    white bread
Custard sauce (recipe follows)
12 strawberries, 12 sprigs mint, and ¼ cup seedless raspberry jam
    for garnish

Heat oven to 350°. Butter 8-inch square baking dish or 8-inch cake pan and dust with 1 tablespoon sugar

In medium saucepan, bring cream to simmer. Meanwhile, place chocolate in food processor and chop finely, 15-20 seconds. With machine on, pour in hot cream. As soon as it is smooth, add ⅓ cup sugar, the butter and vanilla, and the egg yolks one at a time, process just until smooth. In large bowl, combine breadcrumbs and chocolate mixture, stir to blend well. Beat egg whites to soft peaks. Gradually beat in the remaining ⅓ cup sugar and continue beating until they are glossy and stand in stiff peaks. Stir ⅓ of egg whites into chocolate mixture. Gently fold in the rest until no white streaks remain. Turn into prepared baking pan, Place baking pan in a larger roasting pan, and add enough warm water to reach halfway up sides. Bake in center of oven 45-50 minutes, until set and toothpick comes out with only a few crumbs. Remove and let cool on rack 10 minutes. Then invert onto serving platter. Serve warm with custard sauce. Cut pudding in half and each half crosswise into 6 slices. Spoon a bit of custard sauce on each plate, place slice of pudding on top, drizzle about 1 tablespoon of sauce over side of pudding so that it cascades over edge. Garnish each with a fanned out strawberry and a sprig of mint. Stir 1-2 tablespoons boiling water into jam until smooth and runny. Drizzle 1-teaspoon jam over the custard sauce in a wavy pattern. Draw knife through to give it a feathered look. Serve extra sauce on the side.

CUSTARD SAUCE

6 egg yolks
⅔ cup sugar
2½ cups milk
1½ tablespoons brandy
1 teaspoon vanilla

Combine egg yolks and ⅓ cup sugar. Beat until sugar dissolves and mixture is light colored, about 3 minutes. In heavy saucepan, combine ⅓ cup sugar and the milk. Bring to a boil; gradually whisk the milk into egg yolks in thin stream, beating constantly. Return custard to pan, cook over moderately low heat, stirring constantly until it coats the back of a wooden spoon, about 10 minutes. Should register 180° on instant thermometer. Do not let boil. Remove from heat, strain, stir in brandy and vanilla. Serve warm, at room temperature, or chilled. Can be made a day ahead, refrigerated and covered. Makes about 3 cups.

STRAWBERRIES ROMANOV

This is an old-fashioned dessert, but it has held up well, and most people to whom you serve it today will not have had it before. There are endless variations, and you can play with this recipe all you like. The crushed violet candies, for instance, were my own idea, but I like the little bit of crunch they add. Candied flowers are classic, but can be hard to find and making one's own seems like a lot of trouble.

Sugar some strawberries lightly and add the juice and zest of 2 large navel oranges (grate the zest before squeezing the oranges). Let sit an hour or two in refrigerator, then add about ⅓ cup Grand Marnier or Cointreau, mix all very carefully with vanilla flavored whipped cream (add only part of the juices to start, and the rest more slowly, but not so much of it that the whipped cream ceases to hold its shape) Top with a tiny bit of orange zest and the merest dash of Grand Marnier and, if you like, a few finely chopped pistachios. Or, in lieu of the orange zest on top, garnish with candied violets. Or chop up some violet flavored hard candies and garnish with that.

STUFFED STRAWBERRIES

Ideally, you want the really large berries with the stem still attached. If you can't find them with nice looking stems, just some ratty leaves, then slice off a bit of the top, hollow them out as below, mound the filling over the tops and garnish with a mint leaf. I found grating half the chocolate fine and the other half more coarsely (the larger holes on the grater) provided an interesting texture. These really beg for a good Madeira or Port.

12 large strawberries, rinsed and dried
4 ounces Mascarpone cheese
½ teaspoon superfine sugar
A few drops of vanilla
2 tablespoons grated dark semisweet or bittersweet chocolate
Optional: ¼ teaspoon Kahlua or other liqueur

Remove top of each berry and save tops (if they're pretty—see above). With the tip of a paring knife, remove hull and inner core to form a cavity. In small bowl, mix cheese, sugar, vanilla and chocolate and Kahlua, if using. Use a small spoon to stuff the mixture into cavities of berries. Replace reserved tops. Chill and serve cold, with chocolate dipping sauce if desired, 2-4 berries to a plate, depending on size.

NOWELL'S AMBROSIA

For years, the Atlanta home of Nowell Briscoe and his partner Roland Farrar was THE gathering place for writers and book people, and at the holidays, in addition to the sparkling company and lots other goodies, they got to enjoy Nowell's traditional ambrosia. Nowell writes:

"I always make homemade ambrosia on Christmas Eve, with the holiday music in the background. That is the time I reflect on my life and all I have known and loved, while I am peeling, sectioning and slicing oranges. Everyone comes out of the woodwork for this example of my culinary skills, so it must be good! There is no big secret to it. I start out with three or four bags of navel oranges, which I peel, section and put in a bowl, juice and all. Then I add in

fresh coconut and either walnuts or pecans (I prefer the walnuts) which have been chopped. I mix all this up and put in a large container to put in the fridge to stay cold, and before serving each portion, I take a maraschino cherry with stem and place it on top. I used to mix the cherries up in the mixture, but the coconut turned red, so I keep the cherries out of it and use only when serving. Now that is an 'old' Briscoe family tradition, which goes back to my great-grandmother (or rather her cook, who did all the cooking in the family for two generations)."

HOT CHOCOLATE SOUFFLÉS

This is one I thought had to be impossible—really, soufflés that can be made up to 3 days ahead? But the recipe came from a woman I trust. Nothing to do but try it.

As an alternative to the whipped cream, I garnished one of mine with a trio of raspberries and a couple of mint leaves and then dusted with the powdered sugar, and I liked that as well, maybe even better. This will make 4 servings or you can make 6 smaller ones, it's very rich. To test the recipe, I made these in the morning and refrigerated them all. I baked one that evening (probably 6-8 hours later) straight from the fridge, but it took a bit longer, 20-22 minutes, I should say. It puffed up nicely and was plenty tasty. The next day, I gave my friend Todd one and set two out for an hour before I baked them. I had one that evening warm and the other the next night cold, and both were delicious—sort of like light, moist brownies—but they did not rise very much. However, that might be because I forgot to use the cookie sheet. Todd did use a cookie sheet, and also set his out for an hour, and he said it rose spectacularly, and this was a day and a half after I had made them. So, I would say you can reliably do these a day or more ahead and if you do it right, have a lovely puffy soufflé and if for whatever reason they don't rise they still make a pretty dessert—just don't say the word soufflé to your guests and they'll never know the difference. Call them chocolate brownie puddings; it sounds okay and means nothing.

4 (6-ounce) soufflé cups—see my notes, above
About 2 tablespoons softened unsalted butter, to butter the soufflé
    cups
About 2 tablespoons granulated sugar, to coat the soufflé cups
8 ounces top quality chocolate, coarsely chopped, either bittersweet
    or semisweet (I used Scharffenberger, and half bitter, half semi)
1 tablespoon unsalted butter

1 tablespoon flour
⅓ cup milk
3 egg yolks at room temperature
4 egg whites at room temperature
1 teaspoon vanilla
⅛ teaspoon cream of tartar
⅓ cup granulated sugar
2-3 tablespoon powdered sugar for dusting the finished soufflés (optional)
Lightly sweetened whipped cream (also optional)—see my notes above.

If you are going to bake them now, preheat the oven to 375°. In any case, butter the bottoms and sides of the soufflé cups. Fill one of them with the sugar, tilt and rotate it over a second cup until the sides are completely coated with sugar. Repeat until all the cups are coated and discard any excess sugar.

Melt the chocolate in a medium bowl over barely simmering water, or in a microwave on 50% power—I used the microwave, heating for 1 minute, stirring, and repeating for 3-4 minutes, 1 minute at a time—it should still have some lumps when you finish microwaving, but stir it until they have melted also and chocolate is smooth. If you wait until the chocolate has completely melted in the microwave, you will overdo it. Set aside.

In a small saucepan, melt the butter over medium heat. Add the flour and whisk or stir constantly for 2 minutes. Gradually add the milk and whisk briskly until sauce is smooth and thickened, about 2 minutes. Off heat, whisk in 1 teaspoon vanilla and the egg yolks one at a time, whisking briskly with each addition. Scrape the sauce over the melted chocolate and whisk until blended. Set aside.

Beat the egg whites with the cream of tartar at medium speed, until soft peaks form. Gradually sprinkle in the granulated sugar, beating at high speed, until stiff and glossy. Fold ¼ of the egg whites into the chocolate, then fold all together. Divide evenly among the prepared cups, filling each one no more than ¾ full. At this point, you can cover the soufflés and refrigerate them for up to 3 days.

If these are at room temperature, bake on a cookie sheet about 15-17 minutes (if cold, 20-22 minutes), until a wooden skewer plunged into the center comes out moist but not completely gooey or runny. They may puff and crack a bit before they are done, not to worry. Lightly sift powdered sugar over them and serve with whipped cream if desired, or slightly softened vanilla ice cream, or raspberries and mint leaves.

MAKE-AHEAD RUM PRALINE DESSERT SOUFFLÉS

This isn't quite as convenient as the above, but you can make the base sauce hours ahead, and it can be assembled up to 1 hour in advance and left at room temperature, covered, which means you can do it before you sit down to dinner with guests (don't forget to preheat the oven), and pop it in the oven when you are making the coffee.

4 tablespoons each butter and flour
½ cup milk
½ pint (1 cup) whipping cream
⅔ cup sugar
6 eggs, separated
¼ cup dark rum
⅛-teaspoon salt
¼ teaspoon Cream of tartar
Praline (recipe follows)

Lightly butter a 2½ quart soufflé dish. Fold a 12-inch wide sheet of foil, cut 4 inches longer than the circumference of the soufflé dish, into thirds lengthwise. Butter it lightly and place foil collar, butter side inward, around top of dish, extending it 2½ inches above rim and double folding ends to seal.

Melt butter in saucepan, blend in flour and gradually stir in milk. Add ½ cup of whipping cream (chill remaining cream) and ⅓-cup sugar into sauce. Cook to a boil, stirring constantly, and boil 30 seconds—sauce should be very thick. Remove from heat. One at a time, beat in egg yolks. Stir in rum. You can make it to this point well ahead and chill; if you do, reheat the sauce to lukewarm, stirring constantly, before folding in egg whites.

Beat egg whites till foamy, add salt and cream of tartar and beat until they form soft peaks. Beat in remaining ⅓ cup sugar 1 tablespoon at a time and beat until peaks are glossy. Fold ⅓ cup crushed praline into yolk mixture and fold in egg whites. Spoon into prepared soufflé dish and bake at 375° for 30 minutes—center should ripple slightly when dish is shaken; or, if you like a firmer soufflé, bake 35 minutes, test by pressing center top of soufflé with a finger, it should feel set.

Meanwhile, whip remaining ½ cup cream and spoon into a serving bowl and pass with soufflé. Pass remaining crushed praline in a bowl. Serves 6.

For the praline: place ¾ cup sugar in a saucepan and heat over moderate heat until sugar melts and turns amber—watch carefully that it does not burn; once it starts to color, it can burn very quickly. Add ¾ cup sliced or slivered almonds, shake pan until nuts are caramel-coated, and pour out at once onto a greased sheet of foil. Spread thinly with spatula and let cool. When cooled and hard, put in plastic bag and coarsely crush with a mallet until roughly the size of peas.

PUFFY ORANGE DESSERT OMELETS

At one time, dessert omelets were very chic. They are quicker and simpler than their upscale cousins and if you're intimidated by souf-flés, the dessert omelet is a good alternative, which can be sauced as here with an orange sauce, or any of the Dessert Sauces in that section, and will be nearly as much admired as a successful soufflé, if only because nobody today even thinks about an omelet for dessert, so you will get points for originality—and, think about it, it's still just eggs beaten up with air. And nothing could be more forgiving. You might get a raised eyebrow if your soufflé collapses but, really, an omelet? And, in this version, much of the work is done the day before.

5 eggs, separated
4 tablespoons sugar, divided
2 tablespoons flour
1 tablespoon grated orange peel
¾ cup orange juice
2 tablespoons butter
2 tablespoons brown sugar

Combine egg whites and 2 tablespoons sugar in medium bowl. Cover and refrigerate overnight. Meanwhile, in a separate bowl, whisk together the egg yolks, flour and orange peel until well blended. Cover and refrigerate overnight.

To finish, heat oven to 375°. Beat egg whites on high speed 3-5 minutes or until stiff but not dry. Fold into egg yolk mixture. Set aside.

Prepare orange sauce: combine juice, butter and brown sugar in small pan. Cook and stir over medium heat 3-5 minutes or until butter melts and sauce is heated through (you can make the sauce ahead and reheat).

Grease 6 (5-ounce) soufflé dishes or custard cups. Lightly sprinkle with remaining sugar, shaking out excess. Place 1 tablespoon sauce in bottom of each, reserving remaining sauce. Spoon egg mixture equally into dishes. Place ramekins in a shallow baking pan. Bake 15-20 minutes or until tops are golden brown. Serve immediately with reserved warm orange sauce.

POT DE CHOCOLAT

This is another of those recipes that sounds too good to be true. It is rich and creamy and unbelievably simple. I like to garnish with mint leaves, raspberries and, when serving, a dusting of XXX sugar, but just a dollop of whipped cream would be fine too.

Put 2 egg yolks into blender bowl, whip briefly to blend. Scald 1 ¼ cups half and half. With the blender running, slowly add ¼ to ½ cup of the hot cream to the eggs; blend for 30 seconds. Turn off blender, add 1 cup semisweet chocolate chips, 2 tablespoons brandy or rum and the remaining cream, blend at high speed until smooth. Pour into ramekins or cups, 6 or 4 servings, depending on how large you want them, but small is fine, they are incredibly rich. Chill 3-4 hours, garnish as you will.

ICE CREAM

Really, how domestic do you want to be? Buy it, preferably a good brand.

PROF. BEE'S BLACKBERRY SHORTCAKE

Rob Reginald found this one in a very old (nay, decrepit!) cookbook, and adapted it for a modern audience. Best served fresh, but can also be frozen.

4 cups blackberries (fresh or frozen)
¾ cup granulated sugar
3 cups flour
1 teaspoon salt
6 teaspoons baking powder
¼ cup sugar
⅓ cup butter
1 cup milk

1 egg, well beaten
½ cup water
¼ cup powdered sugar (optional)
1 can whipped cream (or Cool Whip) (optional)

Rinse the blackberries and place them in a bowl. Add the granulated sugar, and let stand for at least 2 hours to draw the juice.

In a separate bowl, combine the flour, salt, baking powder, and ¼ cup sugar. Sift the mix. With a blender or by using your floured fingertips (come on, get down and dirty, folks!), work in the butter, milk, water, and egg, making a soft, moist dough. Turn the dough into 2 buttered and floured round cake pans, smoothing the surfaces with a spatula or knife.

Bake the shortcake at 400° for 15-20 minutes, or until golden brown; when done, a toothpick inserted in the center of the bread should come out clean. Butter the tops of both shortcakes, place on a serving dish, and add the blackberries, placing 1 layer of berries over the bottom cake, with another topping the second cake. The berries should overflow the sides of the shortcake onto the platter. The berries between the twin shortcake layers can also be mashed slightly to produce more juice. Top with powdered sugar and/or whipped cream or Cool Whip.

▶ *Dessert Sauces*

RUTH'S VANILLA BUTTER SAUCE

From my sister, Ruth Nance. She's sweeter, but she'll laugh to hear that.

½ cup butter
⅓ cup sugar
3 tablespoons cornstarch
1½ cups water
1 teaspoon vanilla

Melt butter over medium heat; add sugar, cornstarch and remaining ingredients. Cook, stirring occasionally until it comes to a full boil, 5-7 minutes. Boil 1 minute. Pour over ice cream or a plain, unfrosted cake, or whatever. Try it on your boyfriend. Ain't that sweet?

ORANGE WALNUT SAUCE

2-3 oranges
½ cup sugar
½ teaspoon cornstarch
1 tablespoon lemon juice
¼ cup coarsely chopped walnuts.

Grate zest from the oranges (or remove skin with paring knife and cut into small strips). Squeeze juice from oranges to measure 1 cup. In small non-reactive saucepan, simmer juice and zest over low heat 5 minutes. In small bowl, combine sugar and cornstarch, blend into hot mixture. Cook and stir over medium heat until sauce boils and thickens. Add lemon juice; cool. Add walnuts just before serving.

APRICOT SAUCE

Combine in heavy saucepan: 1 cup apricot preserves, ½ cup cold water, and 1 tablespoon of sugar. Bring to boil, stirring constantly and simmer over low heat 8 minutes. Pour into fine sieve and rub through with a large metal spoon (or skip this step if you don't mind the lumps; I don't. Some do). Stir in ½ teaspoon lemon juice and 2 tablespoons Kirsch or apricot liqueur. It will thicken as it cools. If it seems too thick when you are ready to use it, thin with a little more lemon or kirsch.

BRANDY SAUCE

½ cup sugar
1 tablespoon cornstarch
3 egg yolks, beaten
½ cup cold water
1 tablespoon butter
2 tablespoons brandy
½ teaspoon grated lemon peel

Combine sugar, cornstarch, egg yolks and water in top of double boiler. Cook, stir over hot water until thickened, about 10 minutes. Stir in butter, brandy and peel (you can make **lemon sauce** by substituting 1 tablespoon lemon juice for the brandy.

▶ *Diabetic Friendly Desserts*

Here, as promised, a collection of delicious desserts aimed at the diabetic. Not all of them are completely carb or sugar free, but all of them are greatly reduced and can safely be enjoyed in moderation with a clear conscience. I have also tried to make most of them relatively low fat. If you're going to eat healthy, might as well do a good job of it.

Don't let their healthy status deter the rest of you, however. You will find these plenty tasty too.

STRAWBERRY CHEESECAKE PIE

This one is downright decadent.

1 reduced fat graham cracker crust (or make your own, recipe below)
⅔ cup (5 fluid ounce can) evaporated fat free milk
1 package (8 ounces) fat free cream cheese, softened
1 large egg
¼ cup Splenda
¼ cup sugar (or use all Splenda, it's still plenty good)
2 tablespoons all purpose flour
1 teaspoon grated lemon peel
1½ to 2 cups sliced strawberries, or substitute any other fruit
½ cup (about) sugar free strawberry jelly (or match to the fruit) heated

Heat oven to 325°. Place crust on a cookie sheet. Put evaporated milk, cream cheese, egg, sugar, flour, and lemon peel in a blender, cover and blend until smooth. Pour into crust. Bake on cookie sheet for 35-40 minutes, until center is set. Cool completely on a wire rack. Arrange fruit on top of pie and glaze with jelly. Refrigerate for 2 hours before serving.

LOW SUGAR/LOW FAT GRAHAM CRACKER CRUST

1 cup graham cracker crumbs
⅓ cup Splenda granular
3 tablespoons light margarine or butter (50% less fat and calories; I
    use Land O'Lakes)

Combine crumbs with Splenda, and mix in butter well. Put into an 8-
or 9-inch pie pan and press mixture down evenly over the bottom
and the sides (use the bottom of a measuring cup or a tea cup). Put
aside in freezer until ready to fill.

SUGAR-FREE COOKIE CRUST

Follow the recipe in the Pie Crust section above, but use crumbs
made from sugar-free cookies. Be aware: most of these use Maltitol
or Sorbitol, which cause some people digestive problems.

LOW CARB COOL AND EASY PARFAIT

⅔ cup boiling water
1 package (4 serving size) any flavor Sugar Free Jell-O
Ice cubes
½ cup cold water
1 tub (8 ounces) Cool Whip Lite, thawed

Stir boiling water into gelatin mix in large bowl, at least 2 minutes,
until completely dissolved. Add enough ice cubes to the cold water
to measure 1 cup. Add to gelatin and stir until slightly thickened.
Remove and discard any unmelted ice. Gently fold in whipped topping with wire whisk until well blended. Spoon into 6-8 dessert
dishes or parfaits, and chill until firm. Garnish with fruit according
to flavor, or grate unsweetened chocolate on top. Or you can sprinkle nuts or cookie crumbs on top. You can also spoon this into a
graham cracker crust and chill 4 hours or more, to serve as a pie; but
that does add carbs and calories.

BANANA PUDDING

This is not a real-low carb dessert, but at 25 carbs per serving it can follow a dinner otherwise low on carbs. That assumes 8 small servings, but this is rich enough that small servings should suffice. You can reduce the carbs more by using sugar free whipped topping.

12 Pepperidge Farm Chessmen cookies (any flavor, but butter/pecan works nicely)
¼ cup chopped walnuts or pecans
1-2 bananas (I use one, which keeps the carbs down, but that's admittedly skimpy)
1 cup milk, preferably 2%
2 (1-ounce) boxes instant sugar-free vanilla pudding, or use banana flavored
4 ounces light cream cheese, softened
¾ cup fat free condensed milk
1 tablespoon banana liqueur, or substitute imitation banana flavoring
½ of a 12 ounce container of lite whipped topping, thawed

Line an 8-inch square dish or pan with 9 of the cookies. Break up or crush the remaining 3 cookies and combine with the chopped nuts and set aside. In a bowl beat pudding mix and milk just to combine. In another bowl, beat cream cheese and condensed milk together until smooth. Stir in banana liqueur or flavoring. Fold in thawed whipped topping. Fold in pudding mix.

Slice banana(s) over the cookies and top with the pudding mix. Sprinkle crushed cookies or nuts over all. Cover and chill until ready to serve, at least 2 hours.

RASPBERRY CHEESECAKE PARFAITS

This is low calorie but don't hold that against it. It's delicious and pretty and can be prepared well ahead of time. That's all I think you can ask of any dessert.

¼ cup lite ricotta cheese
¼ cup nonfat cream cheese
1 tablespoon sugar
1 tablespoon Splenda
2 tablespoons no-sugar-added, all fruit seedless raspberry spread, melted*

1 cup fresh raspberries
6 tablespoons vanilla wafer cookie crumbs (about 10-11 cookies)
2 tablespoon frozen reduced calorie whipped topping, thawed.

In food processor, process first 3 ingredients until smooth, scraping sides of bowl once. Set aside. Combine raspberry spread and raspberries, stir gently.

Spoon ¼ cup of the raspberries into each of 2 parfait glasses or glass bowls. Top each with 2 tablespoon each of the ricotta mixture, then 3 tablespoon each of cookie crumbs, then the rest of the ricotta mixture, then the rest of the raspberries. Top each with 1 tablespoon whipped topping. Chill at least 2 hours before serving.

*It can be difficult to find the seedless stuff—you can either strain it through a sieve to remove the seeds, or just go ahead and include the seeds, which is what I do.

▶ *Miscellaneous Notes*

Just because I would like to have these in one place so I won't always be looking for them.

Notes on Thickening Agents:

Wheat flour—use for thin soup or sauce, 2 tablespoons per pint of liquid. Heating with acid causes thinning. High sugar concentrations retard gelatinization and reduce thickening power.

Waxy rice flour (mochiko or sweet rice flour), use for frozen or canned sauces to prevent curdling and separation, 4-5 tablespoons per pint; heating with acid causes thinning.

Cornstarch and rice starch, use in sauces, gravies, 1 tablespoon cornstarch or rice starch equals 2 tablespoon flour.

Potato starch and arrowroot are suitable for egg-starch mixtures or fruit sauces where higher temperatures are not desired; temperatures above 176° cause thinning. 1 tablespoon potato starch or arrowroot equals 2 tablespoons flour. Thinning brought about by excessive stirring.

Tapioca, quick cooking, use for puddings, fruit pies, soup, 3 tablespoons per pint of liquid. Stir while cooking; over stirring tends to disrupt particles, resulting in sticky, gelatinous mixture.

Pearl tapioca, requires soaking, otherwise use same as quick cooking tapioca.

Secrets of substitution:

Our mothers, or for many of you, your grandmothers, did not have access to today's supermarket largesse. "Grocery Stores" were smaller and carried few of the items commonly found on the shelves today. This often meant knowing how to substitute something else for an ingredient called for in a recipe. Today that kind of knowledge is not much taught, and for that reason, I've included here some tips on successful substitution. For the most part, you can switch interchangeably.

Allspice—for 1 teaspoon, substitute ½ teaspoon cinnamon and ⅛-teaspoon ground cloves.

Arrowroot—for 2 teaspoons, substitute 1 tablespoon cornstarch.

Baking Powder—for 1 teaspoon, substitute ¼ teaspoon baking soda and ⅜ teaspoon cream of tartar.

Bread Crumbs—¼ dry breadcrumbs equals 1 slice of bread; ½ cup soft bread crumbs equals 1 slice of bread.

Butter—1 cup equals ⅞ cup of oil, or 14 tablespoons solid shortening plus ½ teaspoon salt.

Buttermilk—1 cup equals 1 cup yogurt.

Catsup—see ketchup.

Chocolate—1 ounce unsweetened chocolate equals 3 tablespoons carob powder plus 2 tablespoons water.

Chocolate—1 ounce unsweetened chocolate equals 3 tablespoons cocoa plus 1 tablespoon butter or other kind of fat.

Chocolate—1 ounce unsweetened plus 4 teaspoons sugar equals 1 and ⅔ ounces semi sweet chocolate.

Coffee—½ cup strong brewed coffee equals 1-teaspoon instant coffee in ½ cup water.

Cracker Crumbs—¾ cup equals 1 cup breadcrumbs.

Cream—For 1 cup half and half, melt 2 tablespoons butter in a measuring cup and add enough milk to measure 1 cup.

Cream—1 cup whipping cream equals ¾ cup milk plus ⅓ cup butter (but it won't whip).

Cream—1 cup whipping cream equals ⅔ cup well chilled evaporated milk, whipped, or 1 cup non-fat dry milk powder whipped with 1 cup ice water.

Egg Yolks—For thickening, 2 yolks equal 1 whole egg.

Flour—1 tablespoon equals 1 tablespoon quick cooking tapioca, or 1½ teaspoons cornstarch, potato starch, or arrowroot.

Cake Flour—1 cup equals 1 cup minus 2 tablespoon of sifted all-purpose flour.

All Purpose Flour—1 cup equals 1⅛ cups cake flour.

Self Rising Flour—1 cup equals 1 cup all purpose flour plus 1¼ teaspoons baking powder plus ⅛ teaspoon salt.

Garlic—1 clove equals ½ teaspoon powdered or 1 teaspoon garlic salt (reduce the added salt in the recipe by ½ teaspoon).

Gelatin—¼ ounce envelope equals a little less than 1 tablespoon.

Ginger—1 tablespoon fresh equals 1 teaspoon powdered or 1 tablespoon candied with the sugar rinsed off.

Herbs—3 tablespoons fresh equals about 1 teaspoon dried.

Hot Pepper Sauce (Tabasco, *e.g.*)—a few drops equal a dash of cayenne or ground red pepper.

Ketchup: ½ cup equals ½ cup tomato sauce plus 2 tablespoons sugar, 1 tablespoon vinegar, and ⅛-teaspoon ground cloves; Hunt's is the best brand of Ketchup.

Lemon Juice—1 teaspoon equals ½ teaspoon vinegar.

Milk—1 cup skim milk equals ⅓ cup instant non-fat dry milk powder plus approximately ¾ cup water.

Milk—1 cup whole milk equals ½ cup evaporated milk plus ½ cup water.

Milk—1 cup whole milk equals 1 cup reconstituted non-fat dry milk powder plus 2½ teaspoons butter.

Milk—in baking, 1 cup whole milk equals 1 cup fruit juice.

Make sweetened condensed milk by mixing 6 cups whole milk with 4½ cups sugar, 1 stick butter and 1 tablespoon vanilla. Cook over medium heat for 1 hour, stirring occasionally. Cool. Makes 4½ cups, and can be stored covered in the refrigerator for several weeks.

Mushrooms—6 ounces canned drained mushrooms equal ½ pound fresh.

Mustard—1 tablespoon prepared equals 1 teaspoon dried.

Onion—1 small fresh chopped onion equals 1 tablespoon instant minced onion or ¼ frozen chopped onion.

Raisins—½ cup equals ½ cup cut, plumped, pitted prunes, or dates.

Sour Cream—½ cup equals 3 tablespoons butter plus ⅞ cup buttermilk or yogurt.

Sour Cream—For dips, 1 cup equals 1 cup cottage cheese puréed with ¼ cup yogurt or buttermilk, or 6 ounces cream cheese blended with enough milk to make 1 cup.

Sour Milk—for 1 cup, place 1 tablespoon lemon juice or distilled white vinegar in the bottom of a measuring cup. Add enough milk to make 1 cup, stir, and let sit for 5-10 minutes.

Soy Sauce—¼ cup equals 3 tablespoons Worcestershire plus 1 tablespoon water.

Sweeteners:

Sugar—1 cup equals 1¾ cups powdered, but do not substitute in baking.

Brown Sugar—1 cup firmly packed brown sugar equals 1 cup granulated, but the flavor of whatever you are making will change.

Turbinado Sugar—1 cup equals 1 cup granulated, but it has a heavier molasses flavor.

Corn Syrup—2 cups corn syrup equals 1 cup granulated sugar in terms of sweetening, but never replace more than half the amount of sugar called for in the recipe. Substitution in baking is iffy, but if you have no choice, substitute the same amount of corn syrup, but reduce the other liquid called for in the recipe by ¼ cup.

Honey—1 cup equals 1¼ cups sugar, but decrease the liquid in the recipe by ¼ cup. If the recipe does not call for liquid, add ¼ cup flour. Unless the recipe calls for sour cream or sour milk, add a pinch of baking soda.

Molasses—1 cup unsulphered molasses equals ¾ cups of sugar, In baking, decrease the liquid by ¼ cup for each cup of molasses, omit any baking powder and add ½ teaspoon baking soda.

Tomatoes: see separate table, below.

Wine—for marinade, ½ cup equals ¼ cup vinegar plus 1 tablespoon sugar plus ¼ cup water.

Worcestershire—1 teaspoon equals 1 tablespoon soy sauce plus a dash of hot pepper sauce.

Yeast—1 cake compressed equals 1 package dried.

Yogurt—1 cup equals 1 cup buttermilk.

Tomato Substitutions:

For 1 pound **fresh tomatoes** simmered and seasoned, use 1 (8-ounce) can sauce.

1 cup **canned tomatoes** equals 1⅓ cups chopped fresh tomatoes, simmered.

For 1 cup **tomato purée**, use ½ cup tomato paste plus ½ cup water.

For 1 cup **tomato juice**, use ½ cup tomato sauce and ½ cup water plus a dash of salt and a dash of sugar. If you only have tomato paste, mix 1 (6-ounce) can with 3 cans of water and a dash of salt and a dash of sugar.

Tomato Sauce—1 cup equals 1 (6-ounce) can tomato paste plus 1½ cans water and seasonings.

For 2 cup **solid pack tomatoes**, use half of 1 (8-ounce) can of tomato sauce.

For 1 can (6 ounces) **tomato paste**, use 2 (8-ounce) cans of tomato sauce.

For 1 can (10¾ ounces) **tomato soup**, use 1 (8-ounce) can sauce and ¼ cup water.

If recipe calls for **tomatoes and onion**, you can use tomato sauce with onion.

▶ *Contributors' Index*

▶ Recipe Index

BEVERAGES AND DRINKS

DESSERT SAUCES

DIABETIC FRIENDLY DESSERTS

EGGS AND BRUNCH DISHES

PASTAS AND PASTA SAUCES
(See Also: Casseroles and One-Dish Meals)

PORK

POULTRY
(See also Casseroles and One-Dish Meals)

SAUCES, DRESSINGS, AND SALADS

SEAFOOD

SOUPS

VEAL AND LAMB

VEGETABLES AND SIDES